thesurrealgourmet®entertains

high-fun, low-stress dinner parties for 6 to12 people

recipes, illustrations, images, and faux pas
by bob blumer

CHRONICLE BOOKS

SAN FRANCISCO

to jane siberry: for sharing the adventures and mysteries along the roads we've traveled, and for teaching me the significance of locking eyes when clinking glasses.

The Surreal Gourmet is a registered trademark of Bob Blumer.

Copyright ©1995 by Bob Blumer.
All rights reserved. No part of this book may be
reproduced without written permission from the Publisher.

Printed in Hong Kong.

Blumer, Bob.
    The surreal gourmet® entertains : high-fun, low-stress dinner
  parties for 6 to 12 people / by Bob Blumer.
        p.   cm.
    ISBN 0-8118-0804-1
    1. Dinners and dining. 2. Entertaining. I. Title.
  TX737 .B59 1995
    642'.4--dc20
                                        94-42916
                                           CIP

Distributed in Canada by Raincoast Books,
8680 Cambie Street
Vancouver, B.C., V6P 6M9

10 9 8 7 6 5 4 3 2 1

Chronicle Books
275 Fifth St.
San Francisco, CA 94103

photography: dick kaiser
design: kevin reagan

contents

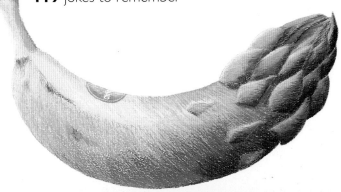

success is this: to laugh often and to love much, to win the respect of intelligent persons and the affection of children, to earn the approbation of honest critics and to endure the betrayal of friends, to appreciate beauty, to find the best in everything, to give one's self, to leave the world a bit better, whether by a healthy child, a garden patch or a redeemed social condition, to have played and laughed with enthusiasm and to have sung with exaltation. . . .

–Emerson

introduction

I have never been fond of proper behavior, formal attire, or tradition for tradition's sake. While others relax with a glass of wine half an hour before the party starts, I inevitably get caught in the shower — albeit with a glass of wine in hand — as my first guests arrive.

What follows is a collage of observations, experiences, and recipes culled from my action-adventures as a host, gallivanting gourmet, and charter member of the "unmonied elite." If I have not "been there" or "done that," I do my best to refrain from addressing, undressing, or redressing whatever "that" might happen to be. It may seem ironic that these musings have been assembled into the rather conventional format of a book on entertaining. But in a world of crystal goblets and recipes for filo triangles stuffed with *foie gras*, who else is going to stand up for your rights to serve dinner on mismatched plates, poach salmon in your dishwasher, or dine like Elvis.

The formula for fulfillment in the Surreal world of dinner partydom is simple: Shop for the freshest available ingredients, master a few select dishes and a killer Caesar salad, buy some spirited CDs, invite a wild-card guest, and train your friends to arrive with fine wine. Follow my suggestions when they feel right but never fear to veer off the egg-beaten path. Missing ingredients, mismatched utensils, and haphazard kitchen gaffs will all melt into comic irrelevance amid the smoke and sizzle of a little spontaneity.

So grab your corkscrew, forget everything the tea and crumpet contingent taught you about traditional dinner party etiquette, and let the Surreal times roll.

partyplanning

So many great reasons for a dinner party, so little time.

Ease into dinner party planning mode by selecting your "cornerstone": a collection of people, cause for celebration, inspiration, or theme. What you choose as a cornerstone will determine the choices you make at each junction as you construct your evening. By starting with whom you want to invite, for example, you can then proceed to design the party around the collection of personalities at hand. Or, pick a date to celebrate and build both your guest list and menu around it. Any which way, a little forethought can make a big difference.

who

invitations Entire books have been compiled on various versions and permutations of the formal printed invitation. But as technology marches on, answering machines have replaced embossers as the conventional method of summoning your guests. Phone messages are fine for most parties, but for special occasions, or specifically themed events, it's fun to establish the spirit in advance with a clever or mysterious invitation.

Whether it's written or oral, be sure your invitation details the date, time, occasion, address, BYO?, and the specific method of torture for non-RSVPing guests. If your guests have children, make it clear if the munchkins are welcome.

Everyone secretly craves to be informed of the appropriate party attire, but no one likes to acknowledge being a fashion victim by asking. Put them out of their misery by casually mentioning it in passing — as though you have no idea they are remotely interested.

guest list dynamics Think of your party as a chess game. To play, you need an assortment of kings, queens, bishops, knights, and pawns. It's the "chemistry" between the pieces that makes the evening work. Too many of one piece, regardless of its rank or "moves," will not lead to checkmate.

In addition to an eclectic mix of personalities, I like to invite one outspoken, controversial "ringer" whom I can count on to invigorate the conversation. I make a mental note of these types when I meet them at other events, and I lure them to my parties with the promise of fine food.

Mixing people from differing woks of life — economically, religiously, ethnically, spiritually, vocationally, as well as those who are single vs. married — can add to the party dynamic if handled with forethought. Be conscious not to invite someone from such a distant planet that they don't have a chance of connecting with the other guests. Also, beware of inviting introverted friends who do not know anyone at the party — they may require more of your attention than you have to give.

There are many ways to spice up a guest list. Share the party with a friend and each invite half of the guests. Invite people you have never entertained before. Or intentionally challenge the gender, generation, or sexual-orientation gap.

In the chess game of life, the triumphant host sends each guest home feeling like a king or queen — *never* the pawn.

send in the clowns On some occasions, it's fun to introduce "new blood" to a party at the point when the energy level typically wanes. If you have invited "vibey" friends who can't attend dinner because of previous commitments, turn a negative into a positive by asking them to come late for dessert or after-dinner drinks. Their arrival will inject your party with a surge of fresh vitality.

neighborhood watch For intimate dinner parties, pacifying the neighbors should not be a concern. However, if your intimate intentions evolve into a massive social event, it is wise not to ignore your immediate neighbors. Inviting them is the old standby. Unfortunately, it's not always desired, or appropriate. An advance note or phone call can work wonders, as will the habit of bringing them goodies after the party, thereby creating a Pavlov's dog effect (put up with the noise, get a treat).

children

> [I like children] if they're properly cooked.
> — W. C. Fields

I have always found that children act most like adults when being treated like adults. This is not to say that you should serve them the same truffle risotto that you are serving your other guests. But if kids are expected at your dinner party, create a party for them that's just as special as yours. Dress up a room they can call their own; treat them to goodies they might not get at home. Rent some movies. Bake some cookies. Roll some peanut butter and jelly wheels. Pop some popcorn. Toss in some arts and crafts supplies and party hats, and leave them to their own devices (avoid too much sugar, or the whole room might explode).

If you are expecting more than a couple of kids, a communal baby-sitter can be a worthy investment. If you don't have kids at home, conduct a quick sweep of low lying surfaces for breakables and sharp corners.

Involve your own children in as much of the preparation as possible (i.e., designing name tags and decorating the room). Then give them an early lesson in strategic negotiating by allowing them to stay up until a designated time in exchange for a guaranteed, unaccompanied retirement. Of course, if they're old enough to help clean up — well, that's another story.

pets Although it may seem hard to believe, not everyone welcomes a pet's "signs of affection" with the same enthusiasm as its master — particularly during dinner. Keep pets elsewhere and feed them before the guests arrive so that they don't nibble on appendages, apparel, or someone's lamb chop.

what

menu planning It's O.K. to be selfish. The first thing to consider when selecting a menu is where *you* want to spend the majority of the evening. If you are fortunate enough to have a kitchen that opens into the living room, and you consider cooking a spectator sport, then starting the meal preparation after the guests arrive is no problem. If, on the other hand, you are the type who prefers to mingle with a glass of wine in hand, a selection of dishes that can be completed entirely in advance might be more practical. A mix of the two, weighted slightly towards pre-prep, is always a safe choice.

I use one fundamental rule when determining how many different items to prepare: Make a minimal number of dishes, but make each one memorable.   A finger food, a salad, and an entree served with fresh bread should be enough to satiate any guest's hunger, as well as his or her palate. The equation is simple:

$$\text{distinctive} + \text{robust} = \text{memorable}$$

menu patrol These days it's virtually impossible to randomly select a half dozen people who will eat everything placed in front of them. The closer one gets to California, the more this rule holds true — and the more the quirk-o-dex goes haywire.   As a person with a few quirks of my own, I have learned to accommodate my guests' eating habits when planning a menu.
Here are the eight most popular quirks and the culprits that set them quirking:

1 The allergy quirk (dairy products, nuts)
2 The health quirk (cholesterol, red meat, dairy products, yeast)
3 The religious quirk (pork)
4 The ulcer/hernia quirk (garlic, hot spices, onions)
5 The politically correct quirk (grapes, veal, the cause *de jour*)
6 The vegetarian quirk (meat, poultry, fish — though, if pressed, many "vegetarians" will eat fish and seafood)
7 The low-fat quirk (butter, oil, cream)
8 The fussy-eater quirk (liver and Brussels sprouts…yuuccchhhh!)

There are two ways of dealing with these quirks. The first is to poll your guests before you set the menu. Do this by including a "quirk questionnaire" with your invitation, or inquiring when they RSVP. Be forewarned: This can be akin to opening Pandora's box. A more manageable solution is to take affirmative action as follows:

1 Avoid the most common offenders. I was once invited to a lavish dinner party where veal — a meat that has the unique potential of belonging to half of the quirk categories — was served. Of the eight people dining, only three finished the meat, while the others ate their veggies and pushed the offending cutlet around their plates. If you plan to serve veal or red meat, it is a good idea to ask your guests in advance whether they eat it.
2 Where possible, add ingredients from the quirk list (i.e., nuts, cheese, meats, etc.) at the last minute. This provides your guests with the opportunity to catch you in the kitchen and ask for their meals to be dished out before the problematic ingredient is added.
3 Prepare extra salad and vegetables so that there will be enough to create meal-sized portions for anyone unable, or unwilling, to eat the main course.
4 If you suspect that your dinner party may turn into a quirkfest, try to prepare a safe alternative — usually vegetable-based, or serve one of my "build-your-own" dinners.

finger foods One or two finger foods will whet your guests' appetite and keep their eyes from wandering to the timer on the oven. Too many can be counterproductive. Last Christmas I attended a dinner party where the host set out a bountiful selection of canapés, crudités, cheeses, and dips. Unfortunately, the stuffed Cornish hens took much longer to bake than anticipated, and what at first seemed like an over-abundance of starters was devoured to the last radish. When dinner was finally served, everyone was too full to eat. Moral of the story: Be frugal with finger foods. If the meal takes extra time to cook, let them starve. They will appreciate your culinary skills all the more if they are hungry when dinner at long last arrives.

bread A crusty Italian or French baguette, served hot from your oven, will improve the taste of almost anything it accompanies. At less than $2 a loaf, it's the ultimate affordable luxury. There is a good old-world bakery in just about every city. Search it out. The trip across town will be well worth the trouble.

   If your bread has lost its freshness, baptize it with a sprinkling of water and toss it, uncovered, in the oven for about 6 to 8 minutes at 300° F, or until it's hot and crispy.

theme-party roulette Theme parties are a tricky — and risky — business. Half-baked themes tend to die slow and miserable deaths. If you're determined to proceed, be sure the theme is a clever one, as well as one that your guests can live with. Then go for it with gusto. Incorporate your theme into the invitations, attire, menu, drinks, decorations, games, music, etc.

   It is inevitable that you may sometimes want, or feel obliged, to invite someone who you know will not be eager to participate. In order to make that person feel comfortable (or less uncomfortable), create an alternate role for him or her, such as sous-chef, bartender, or costume judge. For those who "overlooked" the fine print of the invitation, stock a few simple props (i.e., a funny nose and glasses for Halloween, or a plastic lei for an island theme).

where

When I was twelve, I remember trout fishing in a rowboat with my older, more "experienced" cousin. The subject inevitably came around to girls, and he bragged that he and his girlfriend "did it" frequently in his unfurnished apartment. "How can you 'do it' if you don't have a bed?" I asked in my naiveté. "All it takes is a floor," he responded, with a wise and lascivious grin.

the setting   There is no such thing as an inadequate space for a dinner party. Some of the best dinners I have attended have taken place in cramped apartments, on apartment roofs, on tour buses and yes, even on floors.

 Overcoming the shortcomings of your surroundings will add to the pleasure and spontaneity of the party. Turning an unaccommodating setting into a workable one requires the process of "unlocking" oneself from conventional thinking. If the dining room is too small, move the dining room table into the living room. If you only have two chairs, get rid of them altogether, seat your guests on the floor, and serve Japanese food and sake. Too hot? Eat outside. Too buggy? Make it a safari party and build a tent on the patio from mosquito netting . If all else fails, borrow someone else's place. Some people are happy to lend out their home or apartment as a way to meet people from outside their immediate circle of friends (with the proviso that they are invited, and the cleanup is taken care of).

 To avoid the party-in-the-kitchen phenomenon, make each room as inviting as possible. Keep the lighting flattering, the temperature comfortable, and the stereo volume below the level of conversation. If your guests still don't take the bait, use finger foods and booze to lure them into the desired areas. When all else fails, do as I do and section off the kitchen with yellow police-line tape.

the table   When planning a sit-down dinner, create a table configuration that facilitates conversation and interaction. Round tables are ideal for up to 10 people, after which megaphones are usually required to hear the person sitting opposite you. Long tables also work well — as long as you seat talkative types at the ends. If you do not have a table large enough to accommodate everyone, assemble a patchwork table fashioned out of several smaller tables (your dinner table, card tables, plywood planks, etc.), then mask your handiwork with one or more cloth or paper tablecloths of the same color.

when

party punctuality   Though I have yet to confirm this theory with a Freudian psychoanalyst, it is my firm belief that at the instant we are poised to serve a piping hot culinary work of art, we turn into our mothers.   Suddenly, everyone must be planted in his or her seat at the exact instant that dinner is ready.

 If you love(ed) your mother, but can't quite see yourself in her sensible shoes, build some flexibility into your serving schedule. Assume that your guests assume it is polite to arrive a few minutes late. Inviting habitual offenders half an hour earlier than you want them may be the oldest trick in the book — but it still works.

 Recently I fell prey (along with thirty other guests-cum-victims) to a new and amusing trick. The invitation read "Surprise birthday brunch. Be here by 11 a.m." I dutifully rushed my Sunday morning routine, skimming the newspaper and doing a few chores before arriving at the house just under the wire at 10:55 a.m. As I walked through the front door into the crowded living room, I immediately noticed the supposed surprisee hanging out with the crowd, chatting casually as though nothing was amiss. As I caught his eye, he acknowledged my confusion with a coy smile, and I realized in an instant that the surprise was on me.

 The "surprise party" was a ruse, concocted by the clever host to entice his fashionably late guests to arrive at the party on time. And it worked. Should you decide to try this on your friends, choose the event carefully — you will only get away with it once!

dates worthy of celebration

Elvis's birthday: January 8 (a good day for the All-Elvis Evening, see page 104)

Groundhog Day: February 2

February Blues: Any day of the month

The Surreal Gourmet's birthday: March 6

Ides of March: March 15

April Fools' Day: April 1 (a good day for a Frozen TV Dinner Switcheroo,
   see page 108)

Mardi Gras: The day before Ash Wednesday

Cinco de Mayo: May 5

Dalí's birthday: May 11

The Running of the Bulls: July 7

Lucille Ball's birthday: August 6

Canadian Thanksgiving: Second Monday in October

Sadie Hawkins Day: November 5

First day of each new season: Spring, March 20; summer, June 21; fall,
   September 22; winter, December 21

Longest/shortest day of the year: Longest, June 21; shortest, December 21

Solar events (such as eclipses, comets, meteor showers, falling satellites, etc.)

Last show of any famous TV series (begs for theme food)

why

why not?

how
Just do it.

Sit-down and buffet formats each offer distinct advantages. Sometimes table-space limitations make the decision easy, but often an executive decision may be required.

buffets The advantages of a buffet are: **a)** it doesn't require a large table to accommodate everybody; **b)** it injects a built-in mingle factor; **c)** guests can help themselves to whatever and how much they want without calling attention to their food quirks; and **d)** it can be set up virtually anywhere.

The disadvantage is that the conversation and the party naturally fragment — not to mention that it can be hell juggling a glass, plate, cutlery, and napkin while trying to eat *and* look good, all at the same time.

If you are going to set up a buffet, here are a few hints:

- Be sure that there are enough comfortable places to sit. Import some pillows if necessary.
- Find serving containers that are attractive — even if it is the same pot or pan you cooked in.
- Provide an appropriate serving utensil for every dish.
- Try to serve foods that can be eaten with a fork only.
- For hot food, warm your serving vessels before filling them with food. Whenever possible use a lid to retain heat. <u>Note</u>: Buffets are the only exception to my rule of always warming your plates. I discovered this exception in my early days of entertaining after I heated the plates and then watched in horror as my guests politely tried to keep the scalding china from searing their laps.

sit-down dinners Seated dinners generally require more work, but they often reward the host with a greater sense of achievement.

There are two serving options attached to sit-down dinners. I like to assemble plates in the kitchen. This allows more control over presentation and portioning. Serving "family style" is simpler, and it facilitates individual portion and quirk control. Many of my friends prefer this method, but I feel it transforms dinner into something uncomfortably close to an episode of *The Waltons*. If you insist on the latter, garnish each serving dish and, if you have a round table, get a lazy Susan.

some assembly required One of the easiest tricks to help facilitate mingling involves making a meal that integrates food and activity. I call it a BYO party. No, not bring your own, *build* your own (i.e., shish-kaBobs, see page 68, burritos, see page 70, fondues, pizza, ice cream sundaes, etc.). Everybody loves to assemble their own dinner and the interaction it creates is a great ice breaker. As a bonus, build-your-own dinners are usually good insurance policies against food quirks.

setting up a self-serve bar Choose a location far from the kitchen, put out glasses, liquor, a measuring jigger, mixers, and any available bar accoutrements (see "Bar Staples," page 21). Fill an ice bucket (or wing it with a fishbowl), set out tongs or a spoon, ice down some beer in an appropriate container, cut your citrus, and voilà.

partyprovisions

thetreasurechest

It is satisfying to reach deep into your bag of party tricks and pull a rabbit out of the hat. A well-stocked party treasure chest will help you rise to the occasion of a spontaneous party or rescue a dull one on a moment's notice. Consider adding some of these tried-and-true crowd pleasers to your own personal arsenal:

party store basics Stock up on noisemakers, blowers, poppers, confetti, party hats (you know the party is going well when someone puts one of these on), and some festive napkins. Multicolored serpentine streamers — the kind passengers throw off ships as they leave port — are unquestionably the most festive look that one dollar can buy.

birthday candles Everybody loves the tradition of making a wish and blowing out the candles — even if you don't have a cake. Stick them in anything from the dinner roll to the mashed potatoes.

penny candy Penny candy is one of the great levelers in life. Candy rockets, Tootsie Rolls, Tootsie Pops, licorice twists, jujubes, jawbreakers, red hots, Pez dispensers, etc., trigger warm childhood memories — even if remembering what they used to cost dates you. Sprinkle them about as a table decoration or break them out late at night. In the Surreal world, these confections go perfectly with the finest vintage champagnes.

"bored" games Just knowing that you have a couple of good board games in waiting provides the piece of mind of a million-dollar insurance policy (see page 97).

a bottle of a very special alcohol Great dinner parties are bonding experiences. There's nothing like the after-dinner ceremony of unveiling a bottle from your secret reserve to make every guest feel as close as Mick and Keith. Single-malt Scotch (the experience will be heightened if you claim that the bottle was presented to you by a red-bearded Scotsman with a bagpipe who smuggled it across the Highlands under his kilt), an old Cognac, Armagnac, port, or brandy will be just the ticket.

a bottle of champagne The sound of a popping champagne cork instantly affirms a celebration.

cameras 35 mm, disposable, Polaroid, or video. You never know when a "Kodak moment" is going to pop up. Keep your cameras loaded, charged, and poised for action.

children's games and toys Happiness is a contented child (see page 9).

beverages

Surrule No. 1: Never run out of booze.
Surrule No. 2: Never run out of ice.

The art of the cocktail and the ceremony of uncorking a nice bottle of wine are an integral part of a dinner party. Although drinking may no longer be politically correct, the reality is that many people still savor the pleasure.

wine

For the majority of people, wine is like sex: They've been partaking for years, deriving tremendous pleasure from it, but they still do not come close to understanding all of its complexities.

Fortunately for us, in both cases the fundamentals are simple. Unfortunately, the stigma of selecting "the right" wine can be the cause of great angst. The first step toward selecting appropriate wines is learning to trust your own palate. Make a point of noting the wines that you enjoy. Write down their names or peel off the label. A good place to start is at restaurants that serve "house" wine. These wines are selected because they are good values, have wide appeal, and are easily available.

If you have a mix of fine wines and plonk (wine snob vernacular for inexpensive table wine), serve the good bottles first, while the tastebuds are sober.

quantity If wine is the prime liquid being consumed, a safe range is from one half up to a full bottle of wine per person (one standard 750 ml bottle contains 5 to 6 glasses). Increase the estimate if the party is on a Friday or Saturday. Decrease it if the guest list includes pregnant women, athletes in training, or teetotalers. Err on the high side — leftover uncorked wines are rarely orphaned for long.

color It is courteous to always have some of each wine color on hand. More people tend to drink white than red in the summer. If the entree is something that traditionally calls for red wine (such as red meat), or if the weather is cold, red is usually the color of preference. Despite these guidelines, the only thing you can really count on is that your guests will always drink more of the color you have less of.

preparation Chill all of the white wine (ideally, serve at 45° F). Fine red wines improve after being exposed to the air. Letting a wine "breathe" by simply uncorking the bottle doesn't do much good, because of the limited surface area of wine actually exposed to the air. Either decant the bottle by pouring it slowly into a carafe or pitcher, or fill your guests' wineglasses and tell them not to drink it for ten minutes — good luck!

grand opening Bringing a bottle of fine wine to a party is a bit like bringing a gift-wrapped present. The presenter secretly desires to see it opened. If you sense that a guest has gone out of his or her way to bring a special wine, acknowledge the gift in the kindest way possible — by sharing it.

beer

If the wine snobs haven't succeeded in making you feel inadequate, then the big beer companies will take their turn by insisting that there is a distinguishable difference between the popular domestic brands.

There are three true categories of beer: mass-produced domestic beer, flavorful beer, and light beer. Mass-produced domestics are the familiar names advertised by women in bikinis and guys doing the macho bonding thing. It's a good idea to keep a six-pack of this type of beer on hand in case your guests uncontrollably break into a game of Nerf football in the living room before dinner is served. Flavorful, full-bodied beers used to be the sole domain of imports. Thanks to the recent "microbrewing" revolution, the landscape of flavorful beer drinking has changed dramatically. These traditionally small microbreweries have targeted discriminating beer drinkers (the ones who like their beer to taste like beer). They offer lagers, "pale" ales, etc., which are made in small batches — and in most cases are a pleasure to drink.

Imported beers from around the world are now available in most grocery stores. A few of my personal favorites that are distinctive in taste are Grölsch (Holland), Kirin (Japan), Labatts (Canada), and Bass (U.K.). Stock a variety.

Light beer is a relatively recent invention, but unlike the latest faux "brewing breakthroughs" (i.e., "Dry" beer or "Ice" beer) it actually has a raison d'être. Light beer usually contains two thirds of the calories of regular beer (I have never been able to understand the "less filling" part of the claim) and less alcohol. Women, athletes in training, and people trying to reduce their alcohol or calorie intake tend to prefer light beers. Many of the more flavorful imports have light spin-offs. I recommend these.

quantity A typical beer drinker will drink from 2 to 4 bottles during the course of an evening. Some people will have one beer as a cocktail and then switch to wine.

liquors & liqueurs

In the Surreal world of partydom, wine is perfectly adequate as the sole alcoholic beverage. However, "smart" cocktails before dinner, out-of-the-ordinary concoctions, and after-dinner liqueurs can add an adventurous dimension. If you choose to serve hard liquor, I have recommended (roughly in order of popularity), some liquors and liqueurs to stock. (See page 115).

Madison Avenue will probably have more influence on your brand selection than will your tastebuds. To exercise more of a vote, conduct a blind taste test, or simply look for the best value. Or, swallow the bait and purchase the brand that promises to increase your popularity.

quantity If wine is being served with dinner, most guests will have one cocktail before the meal. As a sweeping generalization, figure on twice as many guests drinking vodka as Scotch or gin. *Note:* It is a popular misconception that a strong mixed drink is a good one. 1-1/4 ounces of hard liquor and 4 to 6 ounces of mixer is a perfect cocktail. More alcohol upsets the balance and kills the flavor — and thus the pleasure — of the drink. If you can't eyeball 1-1/4 ounces, use a shot glass — most bartenders do. One to 2 ounces of after-dinner liqueurs should satiate most guests. If you find yourself pouring more, go directly to "How to Keep Inebriated Guests from Driving Home" (See page 101).

mixers & nonalcoholic drinks

To cover most of the bases, stock orange juice, tomato juice, cranberry juice, sparkling mineral water or soda water, tonic water, cola, un-cola, ginger ale, and their diet equivalents. It is very important to make nonimbibing guests feel comfortable (see page 96). In addition to the standard aforementioned mixers, it is courteous to provide guests with an assortment of flavored mineral waters, fresh juices, and nonalcoholic beers (available in most grocery stores). Adventure Club members should brew up a fruity tea, then add honey, fresh mint leaves, and citrus slices, and ice it down in a festive pitcher.

bar staples

Lemons, limes, martini olives, ice, bottle opener, corkscrew, shot glass, stirring spoon, stainless steel Martini shaker, and strainer.

coffee & tea

Freshly ground freshly brewed coffee is the vice of the nineties. At the end of a long night of food and wine, a strongly brewed French or Colombian roast is a welcome sight. Be prepared — someone will always want decaf and someone else will want tea. Borrowing a second coffee maker for decaf is a good way to serve everyone at the same time. Another option for a back-up brewer is a glass carafe-style "French press," or "plunger." These brew up a great thick cup of coffee. Avoid mentioning that you own an espresso machine unless you're a glutton for punishment. Don't forget fresh cream, milk, sugar, sugar substitute, honey, and lemon.

thepantry

If you plan to host more than a couple of dinner parties a year, it's an efficient and economical idea to stock your party pantry with supplies.

staples Head for your local super discount bulk supply store and buy in quantity. For year-round party giving, stock napkins (cocktail and dinner), dinner candles, mineral waters, mixers, garbage bags, etc. Spontaneous party lovers should stock "green" (extra-virgin) olive oil and dried pasta to mix with garlic, spices, and whatever happens to be in the refrigerator for a pasta *di momento*. If you have your own favorite spontaneous meal, build a cache of its ingredients. Stock stock. A few cans of chicken, vegetable, or fish stock can help you make soups and sauces on a whim. For the BBQ season, go deep on paper plates, charcoal, citronella anti-bug candles, tiki-style candles, etc.

a note on spices There are two types of products sold in grocery stores that are marked up so much that I shake my head every time I pass them in the aisle: spices and breakfast cereal. I'll leave the discussion of the latter for the potential sequel, *The Cereal Gourmet.*

In most grocery stores the cost of a conventional jar of spices (i.e., dried oregano or black peppercorns) runs about three dollars. Down the street at your local natural foods, bulk foods, or ethnic grocery store, these same spices are available by the ounce. What you don't get is the jar and a brand name; what you do get is a savings of up to 500 percent.

inexpensive party luxuries

- **thick paper napkins or folded cloth napkins**
- **coffee made from freshly roasted coffee beans, freshly brewed and served with real cream**
- **an endless supply of bottled sparkling mineral water**
- **candlelight**
- **crusty fresh bread or focaccia**
- **fresh-cut flowers**
- **a small box of fancy chocolates or chocolate truffles**
- **fancy or funky cocktail swizzle sticks or umbrellas**
- **a recently released CD or tape**

serving**apparatus**

Good food transcends the plate it is served on.
— If it's not a Zen saying, it should be

Despite what every kitchenware catalogue would like you to believe, it is entirely possible to serve on mismatched plates and cutlery. Anyone can buy a matching set of silverware and dishes for twelve, but it takes style and panache to compile a table of "found" place settings. This is not to say that a full-on place setting isn't acceptable and attractive. The point is, as long as each guest has a dinner plate, a glass, and cutlery, everything else is superfluous.

In order to stretch what you have to fit what you need, borrow matching units of silverware and plates from friends (they will feel they are getting off easy), or buy stainless steel cutlery, glasses, etc., for a song at a restaurant supply store. If your patchwork table feels too disjointed, distract attention from the components with an eye-catching centerpiece of fresh flowers.

If the mix-and-match approach leaves you feeling inadequate, wait for Christmas and ask Santa for the matching set of whatever you feel is impeding your climb to the next social strata.

"paper or plastic" We should all draw our own line between convenience and snobbery. (I'll gladly eat from a sturdy paper plate, drink from a plastic cup, and wipe my mouth with a paper napkin, but my snob-o-meter hits the red zone at plastic cutlery.) Just remember, caviar on a plastic fork is better then no caviar at all, and champagne from a slipper can taste divine.

rentals If symmetry is the way things have to be, and Santa hasn't granted your wishes, rent. For parties of 12, the cost of delivery is disproportionate to the cost of the actual rental. If you pick up and return the goods yourself, the cost of renting silverware, plates, wine glasses, and coffee cups/saucers is minimal.

foreign accents Despite my constant lobbying to keep everything simple, it's always nice to add a personal flare to your table. Flea markets and garage sales are ideal places to score individual flower holders, napkin holders, or tiny spice dishes. Indian restaurants use these dishes for cumin seeds, caraway seeds, etc. You can also use them for kosher salt, coarse-ground black pepper, fresh herbs (stems off), etc. If you happen across any of these items, buy them for a rainy party day.

cookingutensils

I must confess that after mocking high-tech appliances in my first cookbook, I learned to operate a food processor — and came dangerously close to getting hooked. Someone bought me a mini-Cuisinart (which I promptly hid in a cupboard). I was beginning to appreciate its virtues, however, until karma caught up with me and I smoked the motor while attempting to whip mashed potatoes for twelve.

Moral of the story: Stick with what works for you. A simple assortment of kitchen tools will enable you to prepare everything in this book. Here's a checklist:

8 to 10 quart stock pot with lid

Two 10-inch sauté pans, preferably with a nonstick surface

Assortment of bowls

Oven-proof baking dish

Baking sheet

Blender or food processor

Sharp 6 or 8-inch chef's knife

Cutting board

Colander or pasta strainer

Vegetable steamer

Grill

Pair of long tongs

2-cup-size measuring cup

Standard set of measuring spoons

If you are missing any of these basics, I recommend a trek to your local restaurant supply store, which makes for a great action adventure. (Check the Yellow Pages.) These stores are usually much less expensive than kitchen or department stores, and they offer everything you need, in many size increments. The fear of cooking for twelve will dissipate when you see the industrial-sized equipment they sell to feed hundreds in one sitting. When purchasing pots, pans, mixing bowls, etc., select those that are attractive enough (in an industrial sort of way) to serve from. It's not necessarily a matter of money — some just look ugly while others are more presentable. The presentable choice will come in handy when you find that you've used up all your serving vessels during the course of a large party.

the "facilities"

I consider a bathroom to be clean if there are no wet towels on the floor and the shower faucet is not dripping. However, in order for your guests to pamper themselves in the "manor" in which they have grown accustomed, there are a few common-sense supplies that you should have:

the basics

- An extra roll of toilet paper in clear view.
- A plunger tucked away but noticeable.
- A fresh bar of luxurious soap.
- Clean hand towels.
- A box of tissues.
- A wastepaper basket.
- A respectably sized mirror. (It's hard to check your hair and shoes at the same time in a small round shaving mirror.)
- Privacy. In the absence of a locking door, have a Knock Before Entering sign on the outside.

the adventure club

- Use fragrant flowers such as tuberoses, lilacs, or jasmine, or dried flowers in the form of potpourri, as a natural room deodorizer.
- Light the bathroom exclusively by candlelight. The gentle light spares guests from walking out of a dimly lit dining area into a lavatory that is illuminated like an interrogation room.
- Advanced Adventure Club types may want to fill the tub with water and create a water garden of floating candles, lilies, and rose petals.

the art of ambiance

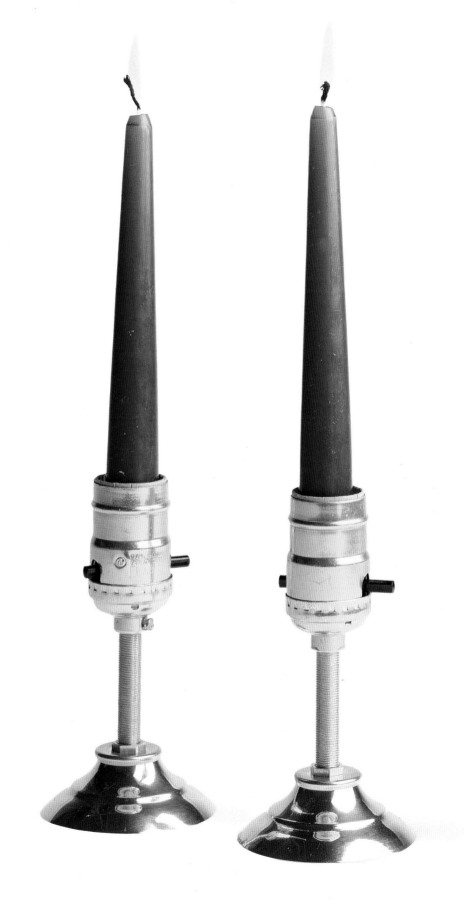

It's exciting to walk into a room and feel that a great party is about to take place. This highly sought-after sensation is triggered by a mysterious "energy" that emanates from a combination of smells, lighting, music, and decor, as well as the "vibe" of the crowd — and most importantly — the host. If a little attention is focused on each of these details, they will project an overall impression that is far greater than the sum of the parts.

decorating&redecorating

Dressing up a room can be as simple as tossing a few serpentine streamers over the chandelier, or as complex as re-creating the Sistine Chapel. The goal in either case should be to convey a sense of occasion and excitement.

Redecorating involves rearranging the existing furniture and fixtures. It is common sense to arrange our home furnishings to suit the number of people inhabiting the space. However, we often forget to reconfigure the furniture to accommodate a greater number of guests. Take a moment to visualize how the room will look when it is full. Will that chair be in the middle of nowhere? Is there a place for people sitting on that couch to put down their drinks?

Of course, the word *redecorate* is also a nice euphemism for "hide the breakables and family heirlooms."

flowerpower

Nothing glorifies a room like flowers, and there is virtually no place in which they are inappropriate. Arrange flowers in the foyer, the living room, the bathroom, as a centerpiece on the dinner table and/or at each place setting.

When you think of flowers, don't necessarily think of the golden delivery man, poised to deliver overpriced long-stemmed roses faster than a speeding telegram. Be creative. Pick from your own garden or a local field. Bring outdoor potted plants inside for the occasion. Use tree branches, tall grasses, wildflowers, evergreen boughs, pussy willows, cattails, etc. If these ideas sound attractive, but it happens to be the dead of winter, take a trip to your flower shop (or farmer's market, flower market, deli, fruit stand, etc.). Buy what you can afford and divide them up into small vases, placing them in various spots around the party area. A single bird of paradise, iris, or sunflower will look great in a tall vase, particularly if you can catch it in the ray of a well-focused spotlight. On the other end of the floral spectrum, a simple bunch of daisies in a coffee pot will punch up a room.

Fragrant flowers such as tuberoses, lilacs, jasmine, and tiger lilies are highly desirable because they deliver an added payload of olfactory pleasure.

lighting

Lighting is so important that some Hollywood stars have clauses in their contracts demanding that they be lit to exacting specifications. In more humble circumstances, the right lighting can cast a calming and flattering glow on your home and guests.

Here are several tips for creating effective lighting:

candlelight The soft glow of candlelight transforms the simplest meal into an occasion. If you are feeling extravagant, light the entire space in which you are entertaining with candles.

Beeswax, scented candles, and/or elegant dinner candles add a nice touch. Inexpensive paraffin utility candles can work beautifully too — and produce the exact same light as their refined siblings. (Avoid putting inferior quality candles that drip on unforgiving surfaces.)

bulbage Try replacing high-wattage bulbs with low-wattage bulbs for the evening. Or replace conventional clear bulbs with colored bulbs. For some inventive illuminance, use Christmas lights, novelty chili pepper lights, patio lanterns, tiki lamps, etc., to accent the room.

track lighting Track lights and spotlights can be great tools if used correctly. Unfortunately, their virtues are often wasted because they are unfocused (i.e., not directed at anything in particular), misfocused (aimed where the sculpture *used* to sit before you rearranged the furniture), or improperly loaded (using "washes,"* instead of "pin spots"**).

You don't need to be the lighting designer for an arena rock show to correct the situation, but you should approach the task as though you are lighting a stage.

Bulbs that fit in your existing track fixtures can be purchased in a wide range of intensities and focuses. Large hardware stores carry a variety of bulbs, and most big cities have stores that sell nothing but bulbs. Create instant drama by changing a wash to a pin spot and accurately focusing it on a vase of flowers or a bowl of fruit or penny candy. You will be amazed at how the illuminated object comes to life.

dimmers Converting a conventional on-off light switch to a dimmer control is about the simplest electrical task imaginable — even for someone like myself who has never even contemplated changing the oil in my car. The dimmer costs about $5, and the only tool required is a screwdriver. (*Note*: remove the fuse *first* , or you'll be in for a shock.) Dining room lights are a prime candidate for this operation. To avoid being a victim of Murphy's Law, do not attempt this less than half an hour before the guests arrive. *Note:* some fancy track-light systems run through a "low voltage" transformer. These systems require special dimmers that must be installed by an electrician.

---

* A "wash" is a bulb that casts a wide beam of light.
** A "pin spot" is a bulb that casts a very narrow and highly intense beam of light.

music

Music enters through the ears but quickly finds its way to the feet, the head, the heart, and the soul. The right music can be relaxing, uplifting and invigorating. The wrong music can be distracting, depressing, and downright annoying.   Sometimes, the only difference between "right" and "wrong" is timing, tempo, or volume.

Select music that helps set the desired mood but doesn't overwhelm the level of conversation. If the last record you bought was vinyl, consider asking one or more guests to bring a selection from their collection. Don't be shy. Everybody loves to be a music "consultant."

Sequence your music so that the mood builds as the evening progresses, and be sure to keep the music flowing. Homemade compilation tapes are another great way to create a specific musical mood. To avoid the inevitability of the music stopping just as you are completing a complicated maneuver in the kitchen, pre-select a batch of CDs or tapes before the party starts, stack them by the stereo unit and appoint a DJ.

When professional club DJs see that no one is on the dance floor, they end the song early and change the tempo. Even if dancing is not an issue, you should exercise the same discretion. Watch your guests, "feel" the room, and go with the flow — making changes to your intended playlist when the music no longer fits the tone of the party.

surreal sound design

Despite the fact that I am tone deaf and embarrassingly untechnical, my friends assume that because I work in the music business I should know why their stereos don't sound as good as they should. On a surprising number of occasions, handicaps and all, I have been able to effect a positive change. In these cases, the root of the problem is not electronics, but rather logic. The solution is invariably speaker placement. There are three basic rules:

height Speakers should always be at least 2 feet off the ground to keep the sound from being "eaten" by the carpet and deflected off the furniture. Use bricks, books, or upside-down pails to elevate the speakers, and place a piece of carpet or foam under the speaker to reduce reverberation.

separation The word *stereo* is derived from the fact that stereos divide sound into two channels and transmit them through two separate speaker cabinets. In the mixing stage of an album, producers create a full spectrum of sound and designate which speakers the various instruments and vocals are to be played through. When speakers are placed beside each other, all of the sounds melt together. When speakers are spread out or, ideally, placed at opposite ends of a room, the separation creates a richer, fuller sound — the music as it was intended to be heard.

direction Amazingly, speakers are often faced directly into a sofa, a wall, or the other speaker. Sound is like light. If it hits something, it is deflected or smothered. Point and place your speakers in such a way that the sound can travel in a straight line to the area in which you wish it to be heard.

If your stereo is in one room and the party is in another, pick up 50 feet of speaker wire at your local Radio Shack for $7, and relocate the speakers per the three basic rules. *Beware*: Loose speaker wires are the banana peels of high fidelity. Tape them down or bury them under the carpet.

See pg. 116 for the "Musical Hardware Wish List."

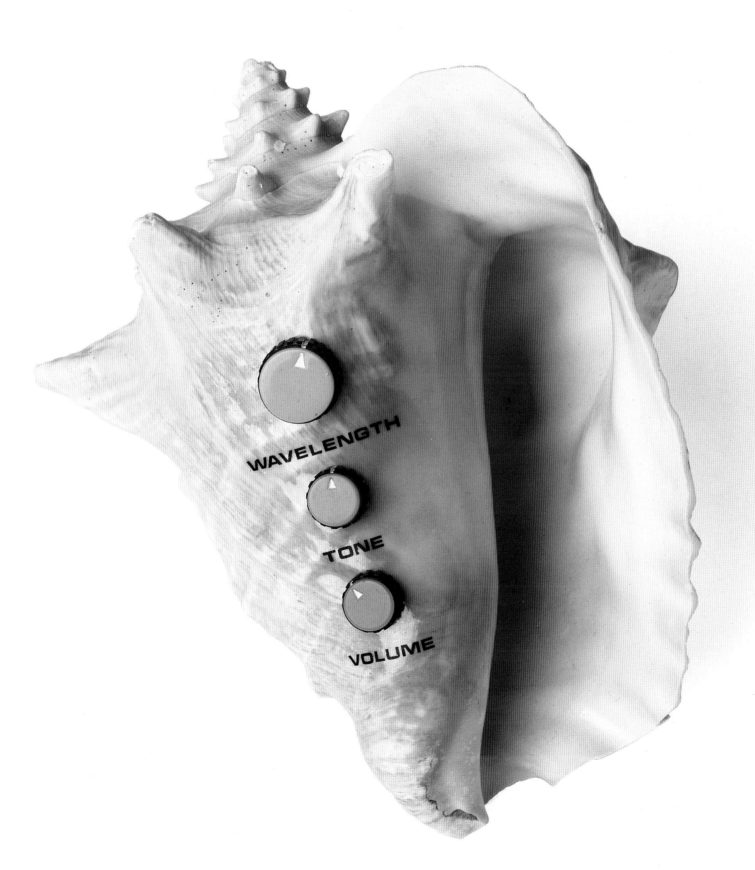

the art of cooking for
6 to 12 people

cookingfor6to12people

menu selection Visualization and pre-planning are the keys to a smooth-flowing and disaster-free evening. Begin by selecting a set of recipes with which you feel comfortable. When creating a complete menu, mix recipes that can be fixed in advance with those that need to be prepared or finished during the party.

A few days ahead of the dinner, spend a half hour during your commute to work (or whenever your mind tends to take cat naps) and focus on the number of guests, the food, the cooking facilities, and the working space in which you will be cooking. Picture yourself preparing the dishes you intend to make and serving them in the manner you have chosen. If the act of visualizing the preceding steps causes butterflies in your stomach, select alternative recipes, simplify the menu, and/or plan to do more of the cooking in advance.

If you are a certified dinner party phobic attempting to overcome your anxieties, select a recipe that can be prepared earlier in the day (i.e., a curry,) and serve it with a simple salad of baby greens. Buy a finger food and a dessert or, more simply still, ask two guests to bring them. In so doing, you can put the mental block of food preparation behind you, and focus on the deep-rooted source of your phobia.

pre-production It is not always possible, and never crucial, to prepare all of the food during the last 90 minutes before your guests arrive, or in their presence. Most of my recipes can be prepared, at least partially, one day in advance. The flavors of some foods, such as soups and curries, actually improve after sitting for a day. Other foods can be prepared in advance and frozen — although I confess to having little experience in this area because the freezer section in my aesthetically pleasing fifties refrigerator functions exclusively as a frost factory.

The corollary to food improving with time is that some foods lose their zest if prepared too far in advance. Before serving any food, taste it. If necessary, "refresh" it with salt, pepper, lemon, and/or a generous portion of the same herbs that were used originally to flavor the dish.

sizing the servings Unless you have specifically asked how hungry individual guests are, it is desirable to make all portions equal. The first phase of portion control takes place when shopping for ingredients. Sometimes a little hardball may be required. For example, if you were to request twelve 1-inch-thick salmon steaks from your local fishmonger, he would probably cut them from a single salmon. Unfortunately, the cut from the middle of the fish can be twice as wide as the cuts nearest the head or tail. There's almost always another salmon "in the back," and you must stand your ground to get what you need. After all, you are the customer and, per the retail credo, that makes you always right.

To avoid running out of food, prepare a little extra — even at the expense of having leftovers. When planning for casual parties where additional guests may drop by, or arrive in tow with your invited guests, it's always wise to prepare extra portions of the main dish. At least be sure to have lots of *something* (i.e., salad, bread, veggies, etc.).

If you are assembling plates for a seated affair, don't let any plate out of the kitchen until you are certain that you have enough of everything to complete the remaining dishes.

timing is everything Having settled on a menu and decided which items to cook in advance, slide back into the visualization mode for a moment and imagine that it's 15 minutes before showtime. Will everything be ready at the same time? Are the garnishes prepped? Did you put the rice on?

Return to the present and create a "critical path" by establishing the sequence in which each dish needs to be started, refreshed, or reheated. When in doubt, scribble out a running order and stick it on the refrigerator.

When showtime arrives, wait until the last minute to put the finishing touch on delicate foods. As a rule, begin steering your guests toward the dinner table before tossing a salad, adding shrimp to a sauce or steaming vegetables.

the accelerated assembly line Assembling a large number of plates quickly is a challenge for professional chefs and amateurs alike. Before you begin, think about how you would like the food to look on the plate, and how the colors, shapes and textures will interact. Create a blueprint in your mind and plan to assemble each plate identically. Then:

- Have all of the food and garnishes ready to be dished out.
- Have the appropriate serving utensils in hand.
- Set the (warmed) plates out on the available counter space.
- Confirm that all of the guests are seated.
- Make up the first plate according to the blueprint in your mind.
- Then, with the help of one or two guests-cum-sous-chefs, dish it all out as quickly as possible, assembly line style. (If you have a cassette deck in your kitchen, play the *William Tell Overture*.)
- Wipe any drippings from around the edge of the plates with a clean dish towel and check that garnishes are in place before allowing each dish to leave the kitchen.

space oddity Oven space, counter space, and refrigerator space are valuable commodities when cooking for large groups — and another reason to keep the menu simple. A shortage of counter space is the most common hindrance in a small kitchen. Sometimes a little ingenuity is required to convert dead space into a functional prepping area. Cover the sink with a cutting board, turn a cookie sheet upside down and place it over the stove's burners (heat off, please) and clear the decks of any appliances or items that are not required for the meal (i.e., the juicer, toaster, bread maker, coffee maker, coffee grinder, kettle, cookie jar, popcorn maker — I think you get the picture).

the grill drill The advent and popularity of propane grills has significantly reduced the inconvenience factor of grilling. If you are using propane, refill your tank before the party and/or keep a spare tank — a party is a bad time to discover the gas gauge is broken.

I still swear by real hardwood charcoal (often available only in mesquite), which I believe provides the best grill flavor. This may stem from my difficulty in conceptualizing how petrified lava rocks can duplicate the smoky flavor of natural wood.

When grilling with real charcoal, light your coals 30 minutes in advance. Extra charcoal may be required to keep the fire burning, but it beats fighting to get the coals lit while your famished dinner guests cheer you on. Never use starter fluids to light your coals. They make food taste like a gas rag, not to mention being one of the worst known air pollutors. Use crumpled newspaper, ideally in combination with the very politically correct starter chimney.

Whether you have chosen gas or charcoal, beware that grilling for 6 to 12 people can require a surprisingly large area of grill space — especially if you have chosen to accompany the entree with grilled veggies. Be prepared to grill your food in shifts, or borrow a second grill so that all of the food can be cooked at once.

help! i need somebody Once your guest list hits the double digits, the sheer volume of people becomes an impediment to merely "winging it." In most cases, guests are willing to lend a hand or even arrive early to help, though occasionally circumstances may make this inappropriate or undesirable. In these cases, you might consider outside help. Help comes in the following flavors: bartender, sous-chef, or general kitchen assistance. Consult a friend who uses help, check the Yellow Pages, or hire the kid next door.

Hiring one person to assist with the prep, cooking, and cleanup can make the difference between enjoying yourself and feeling like the "help" at your own party.

if you can't stand the heat... Throwing a dinner party is supposed to be one of life's little pleasures. But there is work involved. Hard work. Even the most enjoyable parties have their trying moments. Compose your own cooking mantra and repeat it to yourself with Buddhist fervor whenever the inevitable disaster rears its ugly head. Not only will this save you untold aggravation, but it will start you down the path toward an understanding of the true Zen of cooking.

recipes

Cuisinewrite

FOOD & WORD PROCESSOR

ON   PULSE/OFF

a recipe user's guide to the surreal universe

The collection of suggestions that follow each recipe is designed to add a few more shades of color to your cooking palette, and to help transform every meal into a bonafide celebration. See which suggestions work for you and let them inspire your culinary muse.

le secret Most recipes have one key step or component that can make or break the whole dish. If I were at your house while you were cooking one of my dishes, I would uncontrollably gravitate to the kitchen, hover behind you, and extol the virtues of this important tip. "Le Secret" is my way of backseat driving in absentia.

the adventure club There's no money down, no obligation, and relatively little risk. If you have the time, energy, and/or inclination to take any of my recipes one step beyond, follow these suggestions to add the fourth, fifth, and sixth dimensions of exotica, spice, and heat. Adventure Club aficionados should make a beeline for "The Advanced Adventure Club" (see page 102).

garnishes These suggestions are designed to inflate the "presentation value" of your dishes.

suggested accompaniments/suggested appetizers Instead of creating complete meals — which I find rather presumptuous — I have presented a choice of finger foods, soups, salads and entrees that you can mix and match according to your own tastes and whims. In the event that you are cooking on autopilot or looking for inspiration, follow these suggestions for side dishes and appetizers that complement the entree you have selected.

alternatives If there's an easy way to convert a meat dish to vegetarian, create more ingredient choices, or reduce the evil C's (calories and cholesterol), you'll find it noted here.

wine It is with a clear conscience that I acknowledge serving $4 wines at my dinner parties, and even on occasion buying a wine because I am attracted to its label. My suggestions for genres of wine to serve with each entree were made in consultation with a panel of wine aficionados. When two or more of them suggested the same wine, I listened. Within any genre you can either spend four dollars, or sell the farm and shop at Sotheby's wine auction.

music to dine by With each entree I suggest five albums to provide you with an evening's worth of stimulating music, chosen to enrich the spirit of the meal. I picked the number five so that those of you with a five CD carousel (the prefered method of transport to Surreal musical nirvana) can load it up and let it rip. The rest of you with single CD players, tape decks, or (gasp!) turntables should assign a guest to play disc jockey.

guest assignments Guests are always asking if they can help. Most of them don't really mean it and should be graciously guided back to the comfort of the living room, where they can continue to nibble and drink. For those occasions when somebody sincerely wants to help, or when you are in dire straits, I have supplied tasks that even the most bumbling sous-chef can conquer.

cooking apparatus Some recipes require large pots or specific utensils such as a steamer or skewers. Check this section before grocery shopping to be sure you have all of the tools required for the job. Substitute liberally (i.e., any skillet may replace a sauté pan).

serving apparatus An early warning signal for those dishes that require large serving platters, bowls, etc.

hints for advance prep The more you can prepare in advance, the more time you will have to enjoy your own party. These tips will allow you plenty of time to bask in the glory of your culinary creations.

prep time Although everyone slices and dices at his or her own speed, I have provided my best estimate of the time required to measure out, wash, chop and assemble all of the listed ingredients for a party of 6. Preparing portions for 12 should only increase the prep time by about 50 percent (don't ask me to prove this inverted mathematical theorem).

cooking time My best guess for the amount of time that should be allocated from the moment you crank up the heat, until the dish is ready to serve.

miscellaneous notes & nuances

measurements Each recipe includes ingredient amounts for 6 and 12 servings. In most cases I have simply saved you the trouble of multiplying and the need to bring a calculator to the grocery store. But in some cases, the amounts do not increase proportionately. These situations are noted.

All of the instructions are for 6 servings. Any time a step in the cooking procedure calls for a specific portion, I include an * to indicate that you should double whatever is required if you are cooking for 12, or amend accordingly, per your guest list.

If you are cooking for more than 12, think logically about the size of your pots, pans, etc., to be sure that they can accommodate the portions. Cooking times will also vary accordingly.

time & money Surreal food doesn't cost a lot of money or take days to prepare. Any combination of a finger food, salad, and entree can be served for about ten dollars per guest (with the exception of lobster) and be prepared in about 90 minutes of actual kitchen duty.

If you're still waiting for that big check in the mail, throw a "twenty dollar dinner party." This poor man's feast is a variation on a potluck theme. Assign each guest to bring one specific gourmet ingredient and a bottle of wine. The *luck* element is left out of the equation because *you* assemble the meal.

to be or not to bbq Several recipes call for grilling as the preferred method of cooking. An oven broiler will always suffice, but nothing beats the flavor of a grill. Adventure Club types living in northern climates need not limit grilling to the summer months. Use your porch or balcony. If you are fortunate enough to have a fireplace, indoor grilling is a simple yet unexploited solution. Stick a small Hibachi or Weber-style grill in the fireplace, open the flue, close the gate, and forget about the four feet of snow in the backyard (before grilling indoors, see page 112).

eating and driving Several of my recipes call for modest amounts of alcohol as a flavoring ingredient. In every case the cooking time is sufficient to burn off virtually all of the alcoholic content. If the smallest trace of alcohol is undesirable, replace with a nonalcoholic equivalent.

garlicmania O.K., so I use a lot of garlic — but now I have tangible evidence of its popularity. Two days after the 1994 6.8 Northridge quake, I left my quivering house for the first time to pick up some groceries. My cupboard was full of dried pasta and olive oil, but if I was going to be stranded indefinitely, I needed fresh garlic. Surprisingly, after the hordes ahead of me had replenished their earthquake supplies, the market still had bottled water and batteries — but alas, a run on garlic had left the shelves bare.

kitchen fever Any kitchen can accommodate the recipes in this book. If your kitchen is large enough to harbor all of your loitering guests, consider yourself fortunate. But no kitchen is too small to impede you from preparing a great dinner. To compensate for a teeny kitchen, or one that is certifiably dysfunctional, borrow a neighbor's oven or alter your menu to reduce the cooking — but *don't* cancel the party.

nutritional neuroses Sumptuous food and fine drink are just rewards for hard work, regular exercise, and a generally balanced diet.

Virtually all of my recipes are made with unprocessed, unpreserved, fresh ingredients. However, a few of nature's finest gifts such as olive oil or coconut milk are considered "unhealthy" by some, if used in amounts greater than a thimbleful. It is some of these same ingredients that contribute to the instant gratification that great food delivers. Fortunately (or unfortunately), life is not one big dinner party. There are plenty of sensible meals to be eaten, and plenty of time to exercise in between. Be rational, but don't be a frugal gourmet.

surrules

No.1 SERVE HOT FOOD HOT. If you have prepared some elements of the meal ahead of time, reheat them to their appropriate temperature just before serving.

No.2 NEVER SERVE HOT FOOD ON COLD PLATES (except as noted for buffets; see page 15). Warm all dinner plates, serving plates, and bowls in the oven at 200° F for 10 minutes. If the oven is full, warm them under hot tapwater and stack them to retain heat.

No.3 "THE FIRST TASTE IS WITH THE EYES" [Sophocles]. Take the time to present every dish in style.

pear&camembert quesadillas

This unusual combination of ingredients is a great starter for almost any meal, and a *guaranteed* crowd pleaser.
As easy to prepare as *uno, dos, tres.*

servings

6	12	
I	2	lime(s)
1/4	1/2	teaspoon salt
1/2	I	cup sour cream or plain yogurt
4	8	8-inch flour tortillas
2	4	jalapeño or serrano chilies, *seeds and membranes discarded, diced finely*
I	2	ripe pear(s), *peeled, cored, and thinly sliced*
6	12	ounces ripe Camembert cheese, *sliced into 1/4-inch slices* (rind removal is optional, but I always remove it)
I	2	cup(s) lightly packed fresh cilantro, *remove and discard stems before measuring*

1 Zest the lime(s) (see page 113), then juice them. Blend the zest, I tablespoon** lime juice, salt, and sour cream or plain yogurt with a fork until the mixture is smooth. Set aside in the refrigerator.

2 Heat a 10-inch sauté pan or cast-iron skillet over medium-high heat. Place I tortilla in the dry pan for approximately 40 seconds *on each side*, or until it just begins to brown. Remove. Repeat with a second tortilla. (If your tortilla expands like a blow fish, poke it with a fork to release the hot air.)

3 After the second tortilla has browned, leave it in the pan and reduce heat to medium-low. Immediately sprinkle half* of the diced chilies onto the tortilla. Cover with half* of the pear slices. Place half* of the camembert strips over the pears. Top with half* of the cilantro, then cover with second tortilla. Cover the pan with a lid and cook for 2 minutes.

4 Flip the quesadilla with a spatula, re-cover the pan and continue cooking for 2 more minutes. (Don't worry if a bit of cheese escapes and begins to sizzle loudly.)

5 Remove the quesadilla from the pan, let sit for I minute, then cut into 8 wedges (just like a pizza).

6 Fill a small bowl or teacup with the sour cream dip or yogurt and place it in the middle of the serving plate.

7 Serve immediately (you may wait until the second batch is completed, but these are best served directly out of the pan).

8 Repeat the process for the remaining quesadilla(s).

le secret Use very ripe pears and ripe cheese. If the pears are not ripe enough, sauté them in butter over medium heat for a few minutes.

the adventure club Go crazy and invent your own fillings (but if you use jack cheese and avocado, it doesn't qualify for the Adventure Club).

garnish Top the sour cream dip with a dash of lime zest.

alternatives i) Pears may be replaced with fresh papaya, mango, or canned pears. ii) Camembert cheese may be replaced with Brie, or Gorgonzola.

notes   i) Flour tortillas are not a specialty food; they are available in all grocery stores. Sometimes they are hidden in the refrigerated or frozen food sections.   ii) All varieties of pears work in this recipe.

guest assignment   Pear peeler and slicer.

hints for advance prep   i) All of the slicing and dicing may be done several hours ahead of time. Keep prepped ingredients refrigerated. ii) If you slice the pears ahead of time, squeeze the juice of 1 lime or lemon over them to preserve their color.

cooking apparatus   A 10-inch sauté pan.

serving apparatus   A large colorful Fiesta-style serving plate and cocktail napkins.

prep time   Fifteen minutes.

cooking time   Twenty minutes.

* For portions of 12, use one fourth of the ingredients for each quesadilla

** Double for 12 servings

sesame-ginger broccoli spears

This Thai-inspired dressing liberates broccoli from the doldrums of crudité dips and Cheddar cheese sauces.

servings
6   **12**

6	12	
1/4	1/2	cup tahini (available in most grocery stores, natural foods stores and Middle Eastern markets)
2	4	tablespoons hot chili oil
1	2	tablespoon(s) toasted sesame oil
2	4	tablespoons soy sauce
1	2	tablespoon(s) rice wine vinegar
2	4	tablespoons brown sugar (any type)
3	6	garlic cloves, *minced*
2	4	inches fresh ginger root, *peeled and finely chopped*
2	4	heads broccoli, *lower stem discarded, cut into bite-sized spears*
1	1	carrot (for garnish)

1 Place all the ingredients, except broccoli, into a blender or food processor and blend until smooth.

2 Place a vegetable steamer in a large pot, and add 1 inch of water. Bring water to a boil. Add the broccoli, cover, and steam for approximately 4 minutes, or until each spear is bright green and slightly tender–but still crunchy.

3 While the broccoli is steaming, fill a large bowl with cold water and 2 trays of ice cubes. When the broccoli is done, toss it into the icy water (this stops the cooking process). Let cool for 2 minutes, then thoroughly drain.

4 Toss the broccoli in a large bowl with the dressing until the spears are thoroughly coated.

5 Cover and refrigerate until ready to serve.

le secret Fresh broccoli. (Look for a firm stalk with tightly closed deep green florets. Any yellowing is an indication that the broccoli has seen its glory days.)

the adventure club Toast sesame seeds and sprinkle them over the broccoli.

garnish Use a vegetable peeler to cut a few 1/8-inch thick curly strips of carrot. Arrange them artfully in curls over the top of the broccoli (it's a color thing).

alternatives i) Hot chili oil is also marketed as "Mongolian fire oil." If hot chili oil is unavailable, replace with 2 tablespoons* of toasted sesame oil and 1/2 teaspoon* chili powder. ii) Rice wine vinegar may be replaced with red wine vinegar.

notes i) This is a messy finger food (albeit well worth the mess). Have napkins handy. ii) Don't even think about replacing fresh ginger with ground dried ginger. iii) If you are steaming lots of broccoli, do it in manageable batches to ensure even cooking.

guest assignment Broccoli spear cutter.

hints for advance prep i) Broccoli may be cut, and the sauce may be made, a day in advance. ii) Do not steam the broccoli any more than 4 hours in advance. Best when made 30 minutes in advance and chilled.

cooking apparatus A vegetable steamer and a blender or food processor.

serving apparatus A large serving plate and cocktail napkins.

prep time Twenty minutes.

cooking time Five minutes.

* Double for 12 servings

mussel beach

Mussels on the half shell are as exotic and flavorful as they are inexpensive.

servings

6	12	
6	12	basil leaves
2	4	tablespoons fresh thyme, *remove and discard stems before measuring*
2	4	tablespoons fresh tarragon, *remove and discard stems before measuring*
3	6	garlic cloves, *minced*
1	2	shallot(s), *minced*
3	6	lemons, *1* zested, 1/2* juiced, 1-1/2* cut into wedges and reserved for garnish*
1/4	1/2	cup fresh Italian parsley sprigs, *remove and discard stems before measuring*
1/2	1	teaspoon celery salt
1/4	1/2	teaspoon freshly ground black pepper
3	6	tablespoons butter at room temperature
1	2	pound(s) cultured blue mussels, *rinsed, and debearded with a quick tug*

1 Mix all ingredients except the butter and mussels in a small food processor or blender, or dice finely and mix by hand in a small bowl.

2 If using a processor or blender, add the butter. Otherwise, add the butter to the mixture in the bowl and blend thoroughly with a spoon.

3 Place a vegetable steamer in a large pot, and add 1 inch of water. Bring water to a boil. Add the mussels, cover, and steam for approximately 40 to 60 seconds, or just long enough for the shells to open (this is the sole object of the exercise). Remove opened shells and continue steaming any closed shells for 1 minute. Discard any mussels that have not opened by this time.

4 Allow the mussels to cool. Remove the top shell.

5 Set the mussels on a baking sheet (facing up) and spoon 1/4 teaspoon of the butter/herb mixture over each.

6 Place the pan under the broiler on the level closest to the element or flame. Broil for about 2-1/2 minutes, or until butter is melted and the mussels just begin to brown.

7 Serve on the half shell.

le secret Do not oversteam or overbroil mussels.

the adventure club Add a few droplets of Pernod (a licorice-flavored liqueur) to each mussel just before cooking.

garnish Lemon wedges.

suggested accompaniment A Martini.

alternatives i) Butter may be replaced with an equal amount of olive oil. ii) This recipe also works with oysters, but you will have to pray for a pearl in order to finance the difference in price.

notes i) Buy the mussels from a reputable fishmonger on the day of the dinner. Select only mussels that are closed.
ii) Keep the mussels refrigerated. iii) Mussels are best washed and cleaned just before using. They begin to dry out once the

beard is removed. iv) Don't worry if you are missing any one of the herbs. v) If you open a mussel and it looks questionable, give it the smell test.

guest assignment Mussel debearder.

hints for advance prep The butter mixture may be prepared days in advance and refrigerated or frozen.

cooking apparatus A baking sheet, a large pot, and a vegetable steamer.

serving apparatus A large serving plate, a plate for the empty shells and cocktail napkins.

prep time Thirty minutes.

cooking time Five minutes.

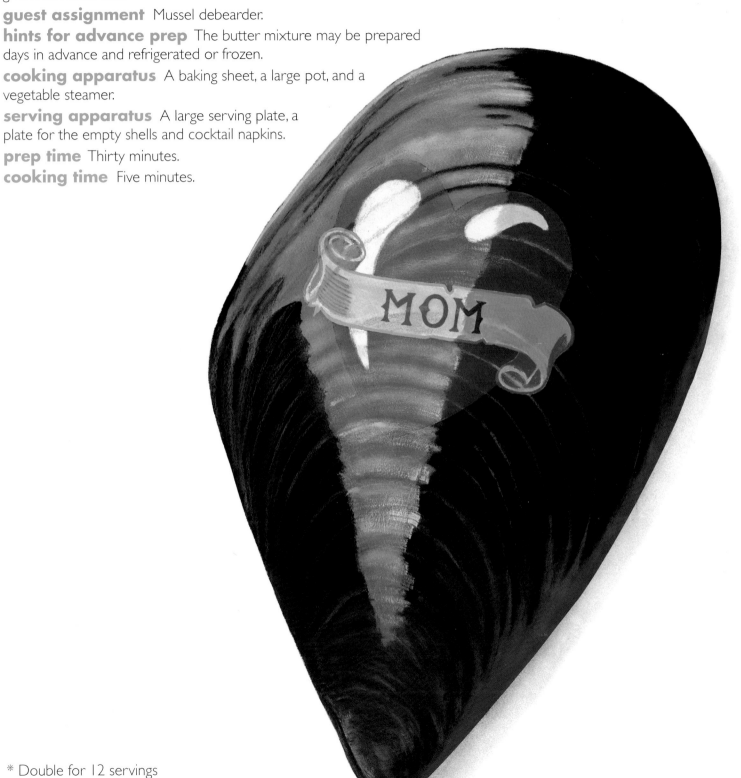

* Double for 12 servings

gratebruschetta

Sometime toward the end of summer, for about two minutes (or so it seems), tomatoes magically develop flavor, texture, and aroma. During this all-too-brief window of opportunity, one should drop everything and pay homage to the tomato gods. Grate bruschetta is the ultimate sacrifice. (Don't be fooled by the simplicity of this recipe — I *promise* you it will win raves.)

servings

6	12	
2	4	medium vine-ripened tomatoes (avoid plastic tomatoes, even if it means making another appetizer instead)
3	6	tablespoons olive oil (best available)
1/4	1/2	teaspoon salt, or to taste
1/3	2/3	teaspoon freshly ground black pepper, or to taste
10	20	fresh basil leaves, *coarsely chopped*
8	16	Calamata olives, *pitted and coarsely chopped*
1/2	1	sourdough baguette, or Italian or French bread, *sliced into 1/4- to 1/2-inch-thick rounds*
2	4	garlic cloves, *peeled*

1 Using the coarse side of a grater, grate the tomatoes into a medium bowl (to facilitate the grating procedure, it helps to cut a thin slice off the bottom end of the tomato and begin grating from that end). After grating each tomato, you will be left holding its skin. Discard.

2 Add the oil, salt, pepper, basil, and olives. Blend thoroughly with a spoon.

3 Toast the bread in a toaster until *very* brown. (If you are grilling, toast the bread on the grill for added flavor. Be careful; bread toasts *very* quickly.)

4 Immediately after removing the bread from the toaster (or grill), rub a garlic clove over the entire surface of one side. Each slice should use up about 1/6 of a clove. (Be careful; when the garlic meets the toast's hot surface it will create fumes that sting your eyes — just like an onion.)

5 *Just* before serving, top each piece of toast with a spoonful of the tomato mixture.

le secret Toast bread until it is brown and crispy. Assemble in small batches and serve immediately so the tomato mixture doesn't have time to soak into the bread and make it soggy.

the adventure club Use yellow or orange tomatoes and/or purple basil.

garnish A big leafy basil sprig.

alternatives i) Basil may be replaced with an equal amount of fresh tarragon, thyme, or oregano. ii) Replace the baguettes with bialy-style bagels, sliced in half.

notes i) When making this for a large group of people, the toasting can cause a bottleneck in the production line. For maximum productivity, borrow a second toaster from one of your guests, or use the oven broiler. ii) If you are lucky enough to have made too much of the tomato mixture, save it and toss with pasta for a delicious instant meal.

guest assignment Toaster and assembler.

hints for advance prep i) The tomato mixture may be prepared 1 day in advance. Refrigerate, then return to room temperature before serving. ii) The bread may be sliced in advance and kept in an airtight bag. iii) The toasting and final assembly takes only a few minutes and should be done immediately before serving.

cooking apparatus A grater and a toaster.

serving apparatus A large colorful serving plate and cocktail napkins.

prep time Ten minutes.

cooking time Five minutes.

citrus-marinated olives

Seasoned olives are the perfect low-fuss finger food. They are also ideal for drive-by visits and cocktail snacks, and to serve alongside fresh sandwiches. Try my selection of spices, or create your own combination from the optional ingredients listed below. Then get with the olive marinating program and concoct a large batch to keep on hand for all occasions.

servings

6	12	
2	4	cups (2 cups = approximately 12 ounces) brine-cured olives such as Calamata, Sicilian Green Colossal, or Moroccan, or ideally, a mixture of them all
1	2	orange(s), *peels grated like a thick zest with the medium grate of a grater* (eat the remaining orange)
1/2	1	tablespoon freshly ground black pepper
1/2	1	tablespoon crushed dried chili pepper
1/2	1	teaspoon fennel seeds or aniseed
2	4	tablespoons olive oil

optional additions

1/2	1	lemon, *cut into small wedges and seeded*
1	2	tablespoon(s) freshly squeezed lemon juice
2	4	fresh rosemary sprigs, *stems removed and discarded*
2	4	fresh thyme sprigs, *stems removed and discarded*
1	2	teaspoon(s) dried oregano
1	2	garlic clove(s), *minced*
1/2	1	teaspoon cumin seeds
1	2	teaspoon(s) coriander seeds

1 "Crack" all of the olives by hitting each one lightly with the flat side of a butcher knife or mallet. (This allows the olives to absorb the flavors.) Some olives are presliced for easy pit removal. These types do not require cracking. In either case, do not remove the pits.

2 In a large bowl, toss all of the remaining ingredients (plus any desired optional ingredients) thoroughly with the olives. Place in a glass container, cover, and refrigerate for at least 24 hours. Ideally, the olives should marinate for several days. Shake the container each day for 15 seconds to mix the seasonings.

3 Mix the olives in the container before serving so that they are covered in the seasoning "debris."

le secret Buy the freshest, firmest olives (and save money too) by shopping at Greek or Middle Eastern markets.

the adventure club Shopping in Old World markets is an adventure unto itself. Sample all the varieties and create a mix of your favorites.

garnish The marinating "debris."

suggested accompaniment Serve with crusty country bread.

alternatives Try different olives and different spices.

notes Yes, this is as easy as it sounds.

guest assignment Pit patrol.
hints for advance prep Refrigerated herbed olives will last for a couple of weeks — and longer without citrus peels or garlic.
cooking apparatus A glass jar with a lid.
serving apparatus A bowl to serve in and a small bowl for the pits.
prep time Fifteen minutes.
marinating time Twenty-four to seventy-two hours.

crusty herbed breadsticks

While the axiom "Surreal men don't bake" generally holds true, men, women, and chimpanzees alike will find these crusty, hot-from-the-oven breadsticks a cinch to make. They're a treat on their own, or as a complement to virtually any meal.

servings

6	12	
1	2	1/4-ounce packet(s) of active dry yeast, or 1* cube (check expiration date. Store in a cool dry place).
1	2	tablespoon(s) honey
1/3	2/3	cup olive oil
1	2	teaspoon(s) salt
2	4	cups warm water (about 110° F)
6	12	cups unbleached flour
1/2	1	cup cornmeal
1/2	1	cup fresh rosemary or thyme, *coarsely chopped. Remove and discard stems before measuring*
4	8	cloves garlic, *minced* (optional)
1	2	tablespoon(s) kosher or coarse sea salt

1 Stir yeast, honey, 1 tablespoon* of oil, and salt into water until it all dissolves. Let sit for 5 minutes. (The foamy layer that forms on top verifies that the yeast is doing its thing.)

2 Place 5 cups* of flour in a large bowl and make a well (a crater the size of your fist) in the middle.

3 Slowly pour 1/2 cup* of the water mixture into the well. Using your hands, mix until liquid is totally absorbed. Repeat in 1/2-cup* increments until all of the yeast/water mixture is mixed with the flour. If mixture is still sticky, add a palmful of flour and fold it in. Continue adding sprinkles of flour until the dough looses all of its tackiness, then knead for 5 minutes. (Knead is bakerspeak for pressing the dough with the heels of your hands, then pushing it away from the body. The dough is then folded in half, given a quarter turn and the process is repeated.)

4 Grease the interior of a second large bowl with 1 tablespoon of oil.

5 Transfer dough to the greased bowl. Roll the ball of dough around the bowl until the dough is coated with oil. Cover the bowl with a damp clean dish towel and store it in a dry warm place (i.e., the top of the refrigerator) for 1-1/2 hours. It should rise and double in size. Pray that it does.

6 After dough has risen, remove it from the bowl and sprinkle a palmful of flour on a dry solid surface. Poke dough with your hand to take out the air (this is known as "punching it down"), then knead it for 3 minutes. Cover the dough with the original dish towel and let stand. The dough should rise again in about 20 minutes. Pray that it does.

7 Preheat oven to 375° F.

8 Brush a large cookie sheet with 1 tablespoon of oil, and then sprinkle a palmful of cornmeal over it.

9 Divide the dough in half. Using a rolling pin or a wine bottle, roll it out until it is about 1/4 inch thick by 10 inches wide.

10 Sprinkle half of the rosemary, garlic, and coarse salt over top, then pat them down so they are imbedded in the dough.

11 Cut dough into 1/4-inch-wide by 10-inch-long strips with a sharp knife.

12 Pick up each strip of dough individually, give it a few twists so that it twirls like a stick of licorice, and place on a baking sheet.* Repeat the process until the baking sheet is full.

13 Dribble a few drops of olive oil over each stick. (This is optional.)

14 Bake for about 10 minutes, or until the breadsticks puff up and brown on the bottom. Then, place under a preheated broiler for 1 watchful minute until breadsticks brown on top.

15 Repeat procedure for remaining dough.

le secret Serve breadsticks immediately after they come out of the oven.

the adventure club Replace fresh herbs with dried Indian, Cajun or Mexican spices.

garnish Rosemary or thyme sprigs

suggested accompaniment A dipping bowl of flavored olive oil, or virgin olive oil, with a pinch of cracked black pepper and/or fresh rosemary.

alternatives Storebought biscuit dough in a cardboard tube.

notes The "lot size" of this recipe is dictated by the size of an individual packet of yeast. You will probably have some dough left over. The remaining dough may be frozen. To use it, thaw in refrigerator, punch it down, knead it and let it rise before baking.

guest assignment Dough roller.

hints for advance prep i) For best results, make dough no more then 4 hours before using. However, dough can be prepared a day in advance and refrigerated. Store in a large plastic bag that can accommodate the dough when it expands. After removing the dough from the refrigerator, punch it down. Knead for 3 minutes and allow 20 minutes for it to rise again.

cooking apparatus Two large bowls, a large baking sheet,* and a dish towel.

serving apparatus Serve in a basket, or standing up in a pitcher.

prep time Fifteen minutes.

rising time Two hours.

baking time Twenty minutes.

* Double for 12 servings

seasoned nuts

The perfect accompaniment for before-dinner cocktails.

cajun peanuts

servings

6	12	
3/4	1-1/2	teaspoon(s) cayenne pepper
1	2	teaspoon(s) dried oregano
2	4	teaspoons dried thyme
1	2	teaspoon(s) garlic powder
1	2	teaspoon(s) freshly ground black pepper
1	2	teaspoon(s) salt
2	4	tablespoons peanut or olive oil
1	2	pound(s) plain, shelled, unsalted roasted peanuts

1 Preheat oven to 350° F.

2 Grind all the herbs and spices together with a mortar and pestle or in a coffee grinder.

3 In a sauté pan over medium heat, heat the oil. Add the spices and stir for 2 minutes to toast.

4 Remove the pan from heat, add the peanuts, and toss until the nuts are coated thoroughly.

5 Arrange the peanuts in a single layer on a baking sheet, bake for about 10 minutes, or until the nuts are golden, turning once.

curried cashews

1	2	teaspoon(s) ground ginger
1	2	teaspoon(s) dry mustard
2	4	teaspoon(s) ground turmeric
1/2	1	teaspoon ground cardamom
1/2	1	teaspoon cayenne pepper
1/4	1/2	teaspoon ground cinnamon
1/4	1/2	teaspoon fennel seeds
1/2	1	teaspoon salt
2	4	tablespoons olive oil
1	2	pound(s) raw cashews

1 Preheat the oven to 350° F.

2 Grind all the spices and salt together with a mortar and pestle or in a coffee grinder.

3 In a sauté pan over medium heat, heat the oil. Add the spices and stir for 2 minutes to toast.

4 Remove from heat, add the cashews, and toss until the nuts are coated thoroughly.

5 Arrange the cashews in a single layer on a baking sheet, and bake for about 15 to 20 minutes, or until the nuts are browned, turning once.

rosemary almonds

servings

6	12	
2	4	tablespoons unsalted butter
2	4	tablespoons fresh rosemary, *remove and discard stems before measuring*
1	2	pound(s) whole almonds, preferably blanched (skin off)
1/2	1	teaspoon salt

1 Preheat the oven to 350° F.
2 In a sauté pan over medium heat, melt the butter. Add rosemary and toss it in the butter for 30 seconds.
3 Remove from heat, add the salt and almonds and toss until the nuts are coated thoroughly.
4 Arrange the almonds in a single layer on a baking sheet, place in the oven and toast for about 15 to 20 minutes, or until the nuts start to crackle, turning once.

i am the walnut

1/2	1	teaspooon ground cinnamon
1/2	1	teaspooon ground cloves
1/2	1	teaspoon aniseed
1/2	1	teaspoon ground ginger
1/2	1	teaspoon cayenne pepper
1	2	teaspoon(s) dried thyme
1/2	1	teaspoon salt
2	4	tablespoons olive oil
1	2	pound(s) shelled walnut halves

1 Preheat the oven to 350° F.
2 Grind all the herbs and spices together with a mortar and pestle or in a coffee grinder.
3 In a sauté pan over medium heat, heat the oil. Add the spices and stir for 2 minutes to toast.
4 Remove from heat, add the walnuts and toss until the nuts are thoroughly coated.
5 Arrange the walnuts in a single layer on a baking sheet and bake for 10 to 15 minutes, or until the nuts are golden, turning once.

le secret Be sure that the nuts are tossed thoroughly in the spices so that they are evenly coated.
the adventure club Make all four and have a nutfest.
garnish A smile.
suggested accompaniment Cocktails.
alternatives Buy mixed nuts in a can and go directly to party purgatory.
notes If you are making more than one variety, do not mix — serve in individual bowls.
guest assignment Nut bowl restocker.
hints for advance prep All varieties may be made up to 1 week in advance and refrigerated.
cooking apparatus A baking sheet. **serving apparatus** Bowls.
prep time Ten minutes. **cooking time** Twenty minutes.

roasted red bell pepper soup

Mr. Campbell, eat your heart out. This light yet robust soup has a distinctive flavor that will never be confused with anything from the soup aisle of a supermarket.

servings

6	12	
6	12	red bell peppers
1	2	poblano chili(es), *membrane removed and discarded, then diced*
2	4	tablespoons olive oil
1	2	leek(s), white and pale green part only, *diced and thoroughly washed*
2	4	shallots, *diced*
4	8	cups chicken stock or vegetable stock, (use canned stock or see page 114)
1	2	medium tomato(es), *quartered*
2	4	tablespoons fresh thyme, *remove and discard stems before measuring*
2	4	tablespoons freshly squeezed lemon juice
1/4	1/2	teaspoon salt, or to taste
1/2	1	teaspoon freshly ground black pepper, or to taste
1/2	1	cup heavy whipping cream (optional)

1 Roast the red peppers and poblano chili(es) whole, over a charcoal flame or under a broiler, turning until entirely blackened (see page 113). Remove from grill and immediately place in a paper bag, seal, and let sit for 5 minutes. Peel off charred skin by running pepper under cold water. (The skin should fall off into your hands. Discard.) Slice skinned pepper open and discard membranes and seeds (each and every seed, or they will end up stuck between your guests' teeth). Quarter the peppers.

2 In a large soup pot over medium heat, heat olive oil, and add the leek(s) and shallots. Cook for about 6 minutes, or until the shallots are translucent, stirring frequently.

3 Add half of the red peppers and all of the poblano chili(es). Cook and stir for 2 more minutes.

4 Add the stock, tomato(es), and thyme. Bring to a boil, then immediately reduce heat to medium-low and simmer for 30 minutes. (Adjust heat as required to simmer.)

5 Remove from heat, add the remaining red peppers (these are added at the end to "goose" the distinctive roasted flavor, which gets washed out by the stock), lemon juice, salt, and pepper.

6 Let the soup cool, then blend in a blender or processor until smooth.

7 To serve, reheat and serve in warmed soup bowls. If desired, top each bowl with 1 to 2 tablespoons of heavy cream per serving, dribbled over the surface in a creative pattern.

le secret Grill peppers over hardwood charcoal.

the adventure club Use orange or yellow peppers. (If available, replace tomato with a yellow tomato or a handful of yellow cherry tomatoes.)

garnish A sprig of thyme.

suggested accompaniment Crusty bread.

alternatives i) Soup may be served chilled. ii) Poblano pepper may be replaced with 2* jalapeno chilies.

notes Common green bell peppers will work perfectly — but the resulting color will be uninspiring.

guest assignment Soup ladler.

hints for advance prep The soup may be made up to 2 days in advance and refrigerated, or frozen for up to 6 months. (Not a bad option if you have some spare time in September when colored peppers are pennies a pound.)

cooking apparatus A grill (optional) and a soup pot.

serving apparatus Soup bowls.

prep time Forty minutes (slightly longer if grilling).

cooking time Forty minutes

* Double for 12 servings

(BELL® is a registered trademark of Bell Sports, Inc.)

vichyssoise with roasted garlic

A *Nouvelle Rustica* variation of the classic recipe.

servings

6	12	
1	2	whole bulb(s) of garlic
1	2	tablespoon(s) butter
1	2	large leek(s), white and light green parts only, *coarsely chopped and thoroughly washed*
1	2	medium cooking onion(s), *diced*
3/4	1-1/2	cup(s) dry white wine
4	8	medium Yukon Gold or Russet potatoes, *peeled and sliced or diced*
6	12	cups vegetable stock or chicken stock (use canned stock or see page 114)
1/2	1	teaspoon salt
1/2	1	teaspoon white pepper
14	28	fresh sage leaves, or 1 tablespoon* dried sage
3	6	cups whole milk

1 Cut off the top quarter of the pointy end of the garlic bulb(s) so that all of the cloves are exposed. Bake in an oven at 350° F for about 1 hour, or until the top is browned and the individual cloves are soft throughout.

2 Melt the butter in a soup pot, over medium-high heat. Add the leek(s) and onion(s) and stir for about 6 minutes, or until they are translucent, but not yet brown.

3 Add the wine and cook for 2 more minutes.

4 Add the potatoes and stock. Bring to a boil, then reduce heat to medium-low and simmer for 40 minutes. (Adjust heat as required to simmer.)

5 Remove the pot from heat and add the salt, pepper, and sage leaves. Let soup cool.

6 Remove the garlic from the oven and let cool for a few minutes. Extract the individual cloves (squish them all out by applying pressure to the bottom of the bulb, or remove them individually with an escargot fork). Add them to the stockpot. (It doesn't really matter if the garlic is added before or after soup has finished simmering).

7 Purée the soup in a blender or processor, cover, and refrigerate.

8 Just before serving, add 1 part milk for every 3 parts soup, and blend in a blender for 15 seconds to aerate. Serve cold in chilled bowls.

le secret Fresh sage.

the adventure club Make purple vichyssoise by using purple potatoes.

garnish Float a fresh sage leaf, or sprinkle diced chives over surface.

suggested accompaniment Fresh crusty bread.

alternatives Serve hot. When reheating, do not let the milk boil.

notes i) The natural starches in potatoes will cause the soup to thicken when refrigerated. Don't worry about it. Blending soup with milk will restore its velvety texture. ii) The recipe makes enough for hearty portions and a little left over.

guest assignment Soup ladler.

hints for advance prep The soup may be prepared up to 2 days in advance or frozen for up to 6 months.

cooking apparatus A stock pot and a blender or food processor.

serving apparatus Soup bowls.

prep time Ten minutes.

cooking time Seventy-five minutes.

* Double for 12 servings

baby greens

Remember the *Titanic:* Steer clear of the iceberg.

Mixed baby salad greens (also known as mesclun) are the trendiest food of the nineties. Packages now available in most grocery stores contain a combination of as many as a dozen different varieties of baby lettuces, baby mustard greens, and herbs. Like gourmet jelly beans, the flavors blend together when they are eaten by the handful. But sample the greens one at a time and you will discover their distinctive flavors and textures.

Baby greens, like their predecessors sun-dried tomatoes, pesto, and goat cheese, were formerly an upscale gourmet product available only in fine restaurants and from gourmet shops (at gourmet prices). And also like their predecessors, their mass popularity is due to the fact that they really are so good. A salad of mixed baby greens, a few accents, and a light dressing is the perfect dinner party staple.

Mixed baby greens are usually sold in 8-ounce packages. Plan on 2 ounces per person. Although they are usually "prewashed," it's a good idea to rinse them in cold water and spin or drip-dry.

Skip the heavier conventional salad staples such as bell peppers, onions, and cucumbers. Instead, combine the greens with one or some of the more delicate ingredients listed below. Toss with one of my light dressings, or make your own simple dressing with specialty oils (i.e., extra-virgin olive oil, hazelnut oil, or walnut oil), and lemon juice or aged or infused vinegars (i.e., balsamic or raspberry).

servings

6 12

12	24	oz. baby greens, *washed and thoroughly dried*

optional additions

(Choose one or more from each group)

cheeses

3	6	oz. chèvre (goat cheese), *crumbled or warmed*
3	6	oz. blue cheese, *crumbled*
3	6	oz. imported Italian Parmesan Reggiano, *shaved*
3	6	oz. Asiago, *grated or shaved*

nuts and seeds

2	4	tablespoons sunflower seeds, *toasted* (see page 113)
2	4	tablespoons pumpkin seeds, *toasted* (see page 113)
2	4	tablespoons pine nuts, *toasted* (see page 113)
1/4	1/2	cup walnuts, *toasted* (see page 113)
1/4	1/2	cup pecans, *toasted* (see page 113)

veggies

1	2	handful(s) yellow, red or teardrop cherry tomatoes
1/4	1/2	cup fennel, *thinly sliced (sautéed, if you like)*
1/4	1/2	cup wild mushrooms, *thinly sliced (sautéed, if you like remove stems before measuring)*

miscellaneous

2/3	1-1/3	cup(s) herbed croutons (see page 113)
1/2	1	leek, *white and pale green part only, thinly sliced or shredded and sautéed in butter or oil over medium-high heat until crispy*
	3	6	garlic cloves, *thinly sliced and sautéed in butter or oil over medium heat until golden brown*
3	6	chives, *finely diced*
12	24	fresh mint or basil leaves

dressings

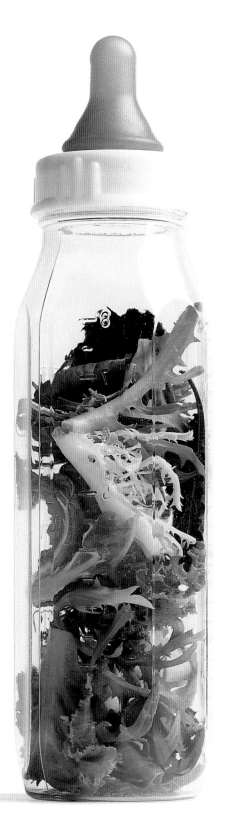

tarragon vinaigrette

servings
6 12

2	4	tablespoons freshly squeezed lemon juice
1	2	teaspoon(s) balsamic vinegar
1	2	teaspoon(s) Dijon mustard
1/3	2/3	cup best-available olive oil
1	2	tablespoons fresh tarragon, *minced*
1/2	1	garlic clove, *minced* (optional)
		Salt and freshly ground black pepper to taste

1 Combine all the ingredients with a whisk or in a blender or processor.
2 Toss greens and any optional ingredients with dressing immediately before serving.

honey-cumin vinaigrette

2	4	teaspoons Dijon
1	2	teaspoon(s) ground cumin
2	4	teaspoons honey
2	4	teaspoons balsamic vinegar
1/3	2/3	cup safflower oil (or olive oil)
		salt and freshly ground black pepper to taste

1 Combine all ingredients with a whisk or in a blender or processor.
2 Toss greens and any optional ingredients with dressing immediately before serving.

le secret Fresh, crisp (cold) greens.

the adventure club Add edible flowers. (See page 112 for a note on how to avoid poisoning yourself.)

garnish "Cheat" the presentation by drawing some of the optional ingredients to the top of the salad

alternatives Make your own mix by combining tender or specialty lettuces (arugula, radicchio, watercress, red leaf, etc.).

notes i) The lettuce leaves should be coated, but not soaked, in dressing. Add the dressing a little at a time to keep the salad from becoming too wet. ii) Wait until the last possible moment before tossing the salad with dressing.

guest assignment Lettuce washer and dryer.

hints for advance prep The salad dressings may be prepared up to several days in advance and refrigerated.

cooking apparatus The optional additions may require a sauté pan, grater, or baking sheet.

serving apparatus A large salad bowl.

prep time Fifteen minutes.

cooking time Varies according to the optional additions.

chez Bob's party caesar

At the risk of repeating myself, I have included this recipe from my first book because it makes people happy. Perfect it and you will find yourself on the "A" list of the party circuit.

servings
6	12	
1/2	1	teaspoon salt
1	2	teaspoon(s) coarsely ground black pepper
3	6	garlic cloves, *minced*
2	4	anchovies (or 1 teaspoon* anchovy paste)
1	2	tablespoon(s) Dijon mustard (the real stuff, not the dried stuff)
1	2	egg yolk(s), *coddled* (see page 112)
1-1/2	3	tablespoons freshly squeezed lemon juice
1	2	teaspoon(s) Worcestershire sauce
1/3	2/3	cup safflower oil
1-1/2	3	teaspoons red wine vinegar
1-1/2	3	medium-large head(s) romaine lettuce, *outer leaves discarded, remaining leaves washed and thoroughly dried*
2	4	cups croutons
1/2	1	cup grated parmesan cheese

1 Add the first 8 ingredients to a large wooden salad bowl, in order, one at a time. Beginning with the garlic, after adding each new ingredient, use the back of a soup spoon to grind it against the wall of the bowl and blend it with the previous ingredients into a smooth paste. It should take about 15 seconds of muscle power to blend in each new ingredient. Yes, Caesar salad making will soon be an Olympic sport.

2 Add the oil and vinegar and blend well.

3 Just before serving, tear or slice the lettuce leaves into bite-sized pieces and add to salad bowl. Toss thoroughly with dressing.

4 Add the croutons and cheese, toss again, and serve.

le secret Use imported Italian Parmesan Reggiano, grated just before tossing.

the adventure club Make your own croutons (see page 114).

garnish Top with an extra sprinkle of Parmesan cheese.

alternatives i) For hot summer nights, elevate your Caesar to cold entree status by adding avocado cubes and cherry tomatoes (preferably yellow) and grilled shrimp, prawns, scallops, or chicken breast (sliced). ii) The anchovy is, of course, optional. iii) I find that the flavor of olive oil overwhelms the dressing so I use safflower oil. Other light vegetable oils or olive oil may be substituted.

suggested accompaniment The salad is self-contained.
notes The lettuce leaves should be coated, but not soaked, in dressing. Adjust the amount of dressing as necessary to keep salad from becoming too wet.
guest assignments Lettuce washer and dryer.
hints for advance prep i) The lettuce may be washed, dried, and refrigerated up to 1 day in advance. (Cut leaves with a knife instead of tearing to avoid browning.) ii) The dressing may be made 1 day in advance and refrigerated in an airtight container.
cooking apparatus A large wooden salad bowl.
serving apparatus Two wooden spoons.
prep time Twenty minutes.
tossing time Two minutes.

* Double for 12 servings

mambo chicken with mango salsa

Trust me on this one. The lime juice and tamari sauce naturally tenderize the chicken, while the garlic and fresh ginger deliver flavor in a big way. Then it's topped with a fresh mango salsa that will make you look like a culinary wunderkind — all with only 25 minutes of prep!

servings
6   12

chicken

6	12	large boneless, skinless, single chicken breasts (see page 112 for chicken handling)
4	8	garlic cloves, *minced*
1	2	3-inch piece(s) fresh ginger, *peeled and grated* (medium grate)
1/4	1/2	cup tamari sauce (or soy sauce)
1/4	1/2	cup freshly squeezed lime juice
2	4	tablespoons toasted sesame oil (very optional)

mango salsa

2	4	mangos, *peeled, pitted, and cut into 1/4-inch cubes*
1/4	1/2	cup freshly squeezed lime juice
1	2	fresh serrano, jalapeño, or árbol chili(es), *seeds and membranes removed, chopped finely*
3	6	green onions, *finely sliced*
2/3	1-1/3	cup(s) lightly packed fresh cilantro, *coarsely chopped. Remove and discard stems before measuring*

instructions

chicken

1 Rinse the chicken thoroughly under cold running water.
2 In a large bowl, combine the remaining ingredients.
3 Add the chicken breasts and turn several times to mix the ingredients. Make sure that chicken is covered by the marinade.
4 Cover and marinate for 2 hours in the refrigerator.
5 Grill on a grill, or under a preheated broiler for about 5 minutes per side, or until cooked throughout. Avoid overcooking.
6 Place the cooked chicken on warmed plates and spoon a generous serving of salsa over each serving.

mango salsa

1 Combine all the ingredients in a bowl and mix thoroughly with a fork. If possible, allow to sit at room temperature for 2 hours to allow flavors to blend.

le secret Select mangos that are at their peak of ripeness, yet still firm.

the adventure club Add kiwis and/or papaya to the salsa.

garnish A lime twist.

suggested accompaniment Sweet Potato Stars (see page 86), or Simple Greens (see page 88).

suggested appetizer Roasted Red Bell Pepper Soup (see page 56).

alternatives i) This marinade works wonderfully with mahi-mahi. ii) The cilantro may be replaced with half the amount of fresh mint.

notes i) When shopping for boneless chicken breasts, choose the plumpest breasts possible, as these tend to remain moister. ii) Make a small incision to see whether the chicken is cooked throughout. If any pink remains, return it to the grill. iii) If red chilies are unavailable for your salsa, use green or dried chilies and "cheat" the color by adding one fourth* of a red bell pepper, finely diced.

guest assignment Grillmeister.

hints for advance prep The salsa may be made up to 1 day in advance, covered, and refrigerated.

cooking apparatus A grill (optional).

serving apparatus Nothing special is required.

prep time Twenty-five minutes.

marinating time Two hours.

cooking time Fifteen minutes.

music to dine by

1 Various Artists *The Mambo Kings, Original Soundtrack* Elektra

2 Sergio Mendes *Sergio Mendes & Brasil 66* A&M Records

3 Stan Getz & Joao Gilberto *Getz/Gilberto* Verve

4 Various Artists *Brazil Classics 1 Beleza Tropical* (compiled by David Byrne) Luaka bop/Warner Bros.

5 Various Artists *Cuba Classics 2: Dancing With The Enemy* (compiled by David Byrne) Luaka bop/Warner Bros.

wine Australian Semillon/Chardonnay blend

* Double for 12 servings

tequila chicken served on corn confetti

A simple, succulent, and colorful southwestern-influenced dish. Do you know the way to Santa Fe?

servings
6   12

chicken

6	12	large boneless, skinless, single chicken breasts (see page 112 for chicken handling)
1/2	1	cup freshly squeezed lime juice
2	4	tablespoons gold tequila
1	2	tablespoon(s) olive oil
1/2	1	teaspoon ground cumin
1/2	1	teaspoon salt

corn confetti

1/4	1/2	cup butter, or vegetable oil
6	12	green onions, *finely sliced*
7	14	garlic cloves, *minced*
6	12	ears of corn, *kernels cut from cobs*, or 3 cups* canned or thawed frozen corn
1-1/2	3	cups of canned black beans, *drained and rinsed* (this is a rare exception where I recommend the canned variety)
1-1/2	3	cups lightly packed fresh cilantro, *coarsely chopped, Remove and discard stems before measuring*
3	6	jalapeño or serrano chilies, *seeds and membranes discarded, finely diced*
1	2	red bell pepper(s), *seeds and membranes discarded, chopped into 1/4-inch pieces*
1	2	teaspoon(s) freshly ground black pepper

instructions
chicken

1 Rinse the chicken thoroughly in cold water.
2 Place the chicken breasts side by side in a 2-inch-deep glass baking dish that is just large enough to accommodate them.
3 In a cup, mix remaining ingredients. Pour over chicken, cover with aluminum foil, and marinate for 2 hours in refrigerator.
4 After the chicken has marinated, preheat the oven to 350° F.
5 Place the ovenproof dish of chicken, still covered in foil, in the oven for 25 minutes, or until the chicken is cooked through and no pink remains.
6 Preheat the broiler. Remove the foil, drain off and discard the marinade, and place the chicken directly under the broiler for about 3 watchful minutes, or until the top of the chicken is browned.

corn confetti

1 Heat half of the butter or oil in a wok or a large sauté pan over medium-high heat. Add the green onions and sauté for 3 minutes.
2 Add the garlic and sauté for 1 minute.
3 Add all the remaining ingredients and the remaining oil or butter. Cover and cook for 8 minutes, stirring frequently. (Twelve servings will take a few extra minutes or require a second pan.)

To serve, cover each warmed plate with a thin layer of the corn confetti and place 1 piece of chicken in the center.

le secret Fresh sweet corn.

the adventure club Sprinkle real confetti over the dinner table.

garnish A lime twist.

suggested accompaniment Sweet Potato Stars (see page 86).

suggested appetizer Roasted Red Bell Pepper Soup (see page 56) or Pear & Camembert Quesadillas (see page 42).

alternatives Replace the chicken with shrimp or sea scallops, or fillets of sea bass or catfish (reduce the marinating time to 30 minutes). The cooking times will vary greatly. Wing it and check for doneness (shrimp should be evenly pink, scallops and fish should be opaque throughout).

notes i) When shopping for boneless chicken breasts, choose the plumpest breasts possible, as they tend to remain moister. ii) Do not overcook corn.

guest assignments Corn husker and kernel cutter.

hints for advance prep Confetti ingredients may be prepped earlier in the day.

cooking apparatus A large wok or sauté pan, an ovenproof glass baking dish, and aluminum foil.

serving apparatus Bright solid-colored plates.

prep time Thirty minutes.

marinating time Two hours.

cooking time Thirty minutes.

music to dine by

1 Ry Cooder *Paris, Texas, Original Soundtrack* Warner Bros.

2 The Eagles *Desperado* Asylum/Elektra

3 Emmylou Harris *Bluebird* Reprise

4 Various Artists *MusicalMeals, Southwestern Cookin'*
Sony Special Products

5 Lone Justice *Lone Justice* Geffen

wine German Halbtrocken Riesling
(German for "half dry")

* Double for 12 servings

build-your-ownshishkaBobs

Let your guests express their artistic inner selves with a palate of multicolored ingredients and a bamboo skewer.

meats

(Select 3 or more of the following)

servings		
6	**12**	
1	2	pound(s) sirloin steak, *trimmed of fat and cut into 1-inch cubes*
1	2	pound(s) boneless lamb leg, *trimmed of fat and cut into 1-inch cubes*
1	2	pound(s) boneless, skinless chicken breast(s) (see page 112 for chicken handling), *cut into 1-inch cubes*
1	2	pound(s) swordfish, monkfish, or yellowtail tuna, *cut into 1-inch cubes*
1	2	pound(s) large tiger shrimp, *peeled and deveined, tail left on*
1	2	pound(s) large sea scallops

marinades

steak Combine 1/2 teaspoon cayenne pepper and 1 teaspoon *each* garlic powder, cumin, dried oregano, and black pepper in a bowl (double the ingredients for 12 servings). Toss the beef in the mixture until evenly coated. Cover and marinate in refrigerator for 2 hours.

lamb Combine 1/3 cup Dijon mustard + 1/3 cup chopped fresh rosemary + 4 garlic cloves, *minced* + 1 teaspoon black pepper in a bowl (double the ingredients for 12 servings). Toss the lamb in the mixture until coated evenly. Cover and marinate in the refrigerator for 2 hours.

chicken Combine 2 *minced* garlic cloves + one-inch piece fresh ginger, *peeled and grated* + 1 tablespoon tamari, or soy sauce + 2 tablespoons freshly squeezed lime juice + 2 teaspoons toasted sesame oil in a bowl (double ingredients for 12 servings.) Toss the chicken in the seasonings. Cover and marinate in the refrigerator for 1 hour.

fish • scallops • shrimp Combine 3 tablespoons freshly squeezed lemon juice + 1/4 cup of minced fresh herbs of choice (tarragon, basil, thyme, etc.), + 1/4 teaspoon salt in a bowl (double ingredients for 12 servings). Toss the fish or shellfish with the seasonings. Cover and marinate in the refrigerator for 30 minutes.

veggies

(select several, or all of the following)

6	12	
2	4	bell peppers (red, yellow, orange, green), *seeds and membranes discarded, cut into 2-inch squares*
1	2	large purple onion(s), *cut into 1-inch slices and separated into rings*
2	4	handfuls cherry tomatoes
1	2	head(s) broccoli, *lower portion of stem removed, cut into 1-1/2-inch spears*
2	4	handfuls mushrooms (one or more varieties, but not bigger than a silver dollar) *stem cut from base of cap and discarded*
2	4	cups of baby potatoes, boiled until cooked through (about 15 minutes)
2	4	yellow Italian squash, *sliced into 1/4-inch-thick rounds*
3	6	ears of corn, *husked and sliced into 1/2-inch-thick rounds*

fruit

1/2	1	pineapple, *skinned, cored, and cut into 1-inch cubes*
2	4	bananas, skin on, *cut into 1/2-inch-thick slices*
2	4	cups strawberries

1 If using bamboo skewers, soak them in water for 1 hour to retard charring.

2 Marinate your selection of meats or fish in their appropriate marinades per instructions.

3 Place each marinated meat or fish, veggie, and fruit in individual bowls and set out buffet style. Instruct your guests to skewer their own kaBobs and place them on the hot grill.

4 Cook for about 10 to 15 minutes, or until the meat or fish appears cooked. Turn 1/4 rotation every 2 minutes.

le secret Cut all the meats and fish into 1-inch cubes so that they cook before their neighboring vegetables burn.

the adventure club Make skewers from foods of the same color (i.e., yellow tomatoes, yellow peppers, squash, potatoes, chicken; red peppers, red tomatoes, red meat; green veggies).

garnish Lemon or lime wedges.

suggested accompaniment Rice and/or Caesar Salad (see page 62)

suggested appetizer Grate Bruschetta (see page 48)

alternatives To save time and energy, use store-bought marinades such as teriyaki sauce, or skip the marinating step entirely.

notes Ten-inch bamboo skewers are available in most grocery stores.

guest assignment Veggie cutter.

hints for advance prep It's always best to cut your veggies just before using. If necessary they may be cut up to 1 day in advance and refrigerated.

cooking apparatus A grill and bamboo or metal shish kaBob skewers.

prep time One hour.   **marinating time** Two hours.

cooking time Fifteen minutes, in the presence of your guests.

music to skewer by

1 Bob Marley & The Wailers *Legend* Tuffgong/Island Records

2 Bob Dylan *Blonde on Blonde* Columbia

3 The Bobs *Shut Up and Sing* Rounder Records

4 Bob Wills & His Texas Playboys *Classic Western Swing* Rhino

5 Barbeque Bob *Chocolate to the Bone* Yazoo

wine Spanish red (ideally from Ribera del Duero)

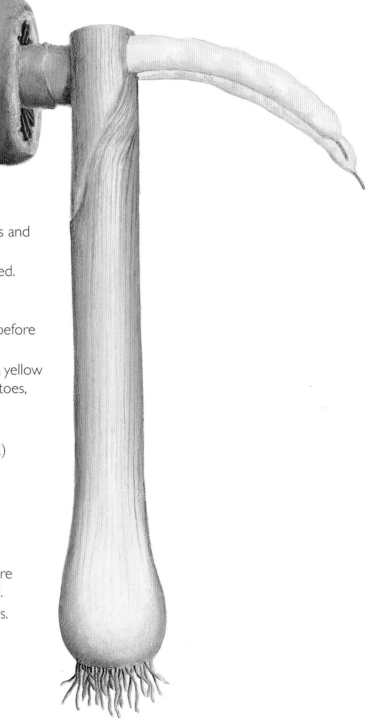

build-your-ownburritofiesta

More fun than a Mexican hat dance (and easier to follow).

servings

6	12	
		## marinated pork tenderloin
1/4	1/2	cup freshly squeezed lime juice
1/2	1	cup freshly squeezed orange juice
1/2	1	teaspoon ground cumin
1/4	1/2	teaspoon salt
1/4	1/2	teaspoon freshly ground black pepper
1-1/2	3	pounds whole pork tenderloin
		## guacamole
2	4	ripe avocados (ripe = indents easily with the firm press of a finger)
1/2	1	cup lightly packed cilantro, *finely chopped with stems removed and discarded before measuring*
1	2	dried red hot chili pepper(s), *crushed* or 1/2 teaspoon* dried red pepper flakes
2	4	tablespoons freshly squeezed lemon juice
4	8	green onions, *finely chopped*
1	2	teaspoon(s) freshly ground black pepper
1/4	1/2	teaspoon salt
1/8	1/4	teaspoon cayenne pepper (optional)
1	2	garlic clove(s), *minced* (optional)
		## tomato salsa fresca
1	2	pound(s) ripe tomatoes, *diced*
1/4	1/2	cup red onion or green onion, *finely chopped*
1/2	1	cup lightly packed fresh cilantro, *finely chopped* *Remove and discard stems before measuring*
1	2	garlic clove(s), *minced*
1	2	jalapeño or serrano chilli(es), *seeds and membranes discarded, minced*
1	2	tablespoon(s) olive oil
2	4	tablespoons freshly squeezed lime juice
		salt and pepper to taste
		## additional condiments
2	4	cups lightly packed fresh cilantro, *stems removed and discarded before measuring*
5	10	green onions, *finely sliced*
1	2	cup(s) sour cream
8	16	ounces sharp cheddar or jack cheese, *grated*
12	24	10-inch flour and/or corn tortillas (or taco shells if you can bear the aggravation of them constantly breaking)

instructions
marinated pork tenderloin

1 In a baking dish or shallow bowl, mix all of the juices and seasonings. Place the tenderloin(s) in the marinade so that the meat is covered with the marinade.

2 Cover and marinate for 2 hours in the refrigerator.

3 Grill the tenderloin on a grill or under a preheated broiler for about 8 minutes on each side, or until cooked throughout (see page 112). Avoid overcooking.

4 Cut the tenderloin into thin slices.

guacamole

1 Cut the avocados in half lengthwise, remove the pits and scoop the flesh out of the peels.

2 Add all ingredients in a bowl. Blend with a fork until the mixture is just slightly lumpy.

tomato salsa fresca

1 Combine all the ingredients in a bowl. If possible, let sit for 1 hour to allow flavors to blend.

tortilla shells

1 Wrap the tortillas (or taco shells) in aluminum foil and warm them in a preheated 250° F oven for 20 minutes.

To serve, place the sliced tenderloin, salsa, guacamole, and the additional condiments in individual bowls and set them out. Guests should be instructed to take a tortilla, add meat and a bit of everything else, then roll the tortilla around the contents.

le secret Use fresh ingredients and ripe tomatoes and avocados

the adventure club Replace the pork with shark steaks (follow the pork marinating and cooking instructions, but halve the marinating and cooking times).

garnish Top the sour cream with lime zest and garnish the sliced pork with a sprig of cilantro.

suggested accompaniments Jalapeño Corn Bread (see page 115) and/or Caesar Salad (see page 62).

suggested appetizer Pear & Camembert Quesadillas (see page 42).

alternatives i) To save time, use the best-available, store bought salsa or guacamole. ii) Pork is the traditional burrito meat, but you may replace it, or supplement it, with steak or chicken. For chicken, use the same marinade. For steak, rub with a mixture of 1 teaspoon* salt, 1 teaspoon* black pepper, and 1 teaspoon* cumin. iii) Sour cream may be replaced with plain yogurt.

notes I have listed the ingredients separately on the assumption that you might use store bought guacamole or salsa. If you make everything fresh, collate the ingredients the recipes have in common so that you do not go in circles at the grocery store.

guest assignment Slicing and dicing.

hints for advance prep i) The salsa may be made up to 1 day in advance and refrigerated. ii) The guac may also be made 1 day in advance, but it is at its best when made 2 to 4 hours in advance. Squeeze lemon juice over it to preserve its color.

cooking apparatus A grill (optional) and an ovenproof baking dish.   **serving apparatus** Eight colorful bowls.

prep time One hour.   **marinating time** Two hours.   **cooking time** Twenty minutes.

music to dine by

1 Los Lobos *KIKO* Slash/Warner Bros.

2 The Texas Tornados *Los Texas Tornados* Warner Bros.

3 Flaco Jimenez *Partners* Reprise/Warner Bros.

4 Mariachi Reyes del Aserradero *Songs from Jalisco* Corason/Rounder

5 The Flying Burrito Brothers *Farther Along: The Best of the Flying Burrito Brothers* A&M Records

wine Mexican beer or Margaritas   * Double for 12 servings

pasta prima donna

Don't be fooled by the common heritage of its ingredients — this dish was born to be a real star.
Mr. DeMille, I'm ready for my pasta now.

servings

6	12	
2	4	Japanese eggplants, *ends discarded and sliced in half lengthwise*
1	2	yellow Italian squash, *ends discarded and sliced in half lengthwise*
1	2	leek(s), white and pale green parts only, *sliced in half lengthwise and thoroughly washed* (leave the bottom root end on to hold it together)
1	2	handful(s) cherry tomatoes, *stemmed*
1	2	head(s) broccoli, *lower portion of stem removed and discarded, cut into large 4-inch spears*
1	2	orange, yellow, or red bell pepper(s)
8	16	garlic cloves, *skin removed*
1	2	cup(s) of extra-virgin olive oil (1/3 cup* for veggies, 2/3 cup* for pasta)
1/4	1/2	teaspoon salt
12	24	ounces of dried fusilli pasta, or double the amount of fresh pasta (fusilli is best, because it "holds" the ingredients better, but any shape or kind will work)
1-1/2	3	cups lightly packed basil leaves, *coarsely chopped*
1/2	1	cup pine nuts, *toasted* (see page 113)
2	4	small dried red chili peppers, *finely chopped*, or 1 teaspoon* dried red pepper flakes
1	2	cup(s) grated Parmesan cheese
1	2	teaspoon(s) coarsely ground black pepper

1 Brush the vegetables lightly with olive oil.

2 Place garlic cloves on a piece of tin foil, dribble 1 tablespoon of oil over them and seal the foil.

3 Cover the grill and cook vegetables for approximately fifteen minutes, or until they are nicely browned on all sides (except for the bell pepper(s) which should be grilled until entirely blackened). Grill the garlic for twenty minutes. Turn vegetables every three minutes or so. After a few minutes on the grill, spread the leek out like a fan to brown all of the layers evenly. The tomatoes and eggplant will cook the fastest. Remove them when they are done.

4 Cut the eggplant, squash, leeks, and broccoli into 1/2-inch pieces. Mince the garlic. Place the bell pepper(s) in a paper bag, seal, and let sit for 5 minutes. Then peel off the charred skin by running pepper(s) under cold water. (The skin should fall of into your hands.) Discard. Cut the pepper(s) open and discard seeds and membranes. Slice the pepper(s) into long 1/4-inch strips.

5 Bring 12* cups of salted water to a boil and cook the pasta according to directions on the package.

6 Warm a large serving bowl and place the chopped veggies, garlic, tomatoes, bell pepper(s), basil, pine nuts, and chilies at the bottom.

7 Drain pasta and add to bowl.

8 Add the Parmesan cheese, black pepper, and the remaining 2/3 cup* olive oil. Toss thoroughly. Serve immediately.

le secret The more herbs and vegetables, the merrier.

the adventure club Throw caution and calorie counting to the winds and add 50 percent more olive oil and Parmesan cheese.

garnish A sprinkle of Parmesan and a sprig of basil.

suggested accompaniment Crusty bread and a Caesar salad.

suggested appetizer Bruschetta or marinated olives.

alternatives Any vegetable may be omitted or substituted.

notes i) Grilled broccoli may sound unusual, but it provides the surprising flavor burst essential to this recipe. ii) Use a robust green olive oil.

guest assignment Grillmeister and pasta boiler.

hints for advance prep i) The vegetables may be prepped and grilled earlier in the day. Reheat in the oven before tossing with pasta. ii) The remaining ingredients may be prepped earlier so that all ingredients can simply be tossed with the hot pasta at showtime. iii) The entire dish may also be prepared 1 day in advance and served as a cold pasta. The extra day allows the grill flavor of the veggies to permeate the pasta.

cooking apparatus A grill, a pasta pot, and aluminum foil.   **serving apparatus** A large festive bowl.

prep time Thirty minutes.   **cooking time** Forty minutes.

music to dine by

1 Diana Ross & the Supremes *Every Great #1 Hit*   Motown
2 Annie Lennox *Diva* Arista/BMG
3 Jane Siberry *When I Was A Boy*   Reprise
4 Kiri te Kanawa *Songs of Inspiration*   London
5 Madonna *Bedtime Stories* Sire/Warner Bros.

wine Oregon Pinot Noir

* Double for 12 servings

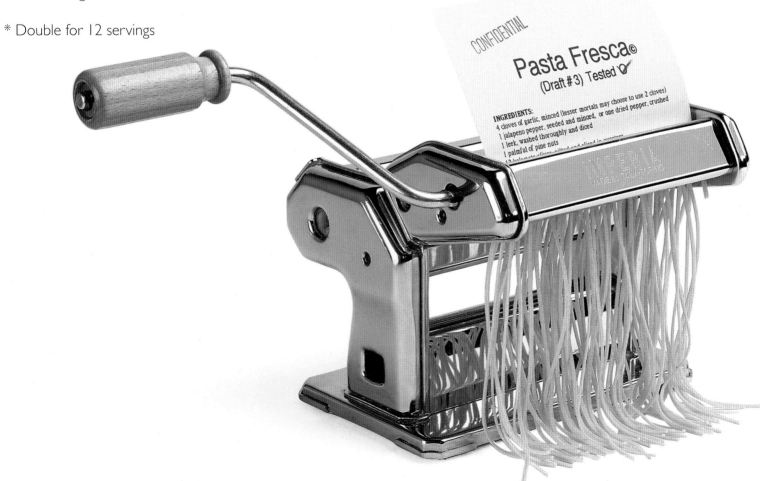

CONFIDENTIAL

Pasta Fresca©

(Draft # 3) Tested ☑

INGREDIENTS:
4 cloves of garlic, minced (lesser mortals may choose to use 2 cloves)
1 jalapeno pepper, seeded and minced, or one dried pepper, crushed
1 leek, washed thoroughly and diced
1 palmful of pine nuts

champagne risotto with asparagus, wild mushrooms, and gorgonzola

Somewhere during its four-century-old history, risotto was falsely labeled as a temperamental food that required constant stirring and undivided attention. In truth, risotto is relatively simple to make and quite forgiving — in fact, almost indestructible — but don't spoil the myth for your guests.

servings

6	12	
1/4	1/2	cup olive oil
4	8	garlic cloves, *minced*
1/2	1	leek, white and pale green parts only, *finely diced and thoroughly washed*
2	4	cups Arborio rice (available in most grocery stores) or short-grain white rice
5-1/2	11	cups chicken or vegetable stock (use canned stock or see page 114)
1	2	pound(s) asparagus, *bottom third cut off and discarded, remainder cut into 1/2-inch-thick diagonal slices*
4	8	ounces of chanterell, oyster, porcini, or shiitake mushrooms (discard shiitake stems, keep others), *cut into 1/8-inch-thick strips*
1-1/2	3	cups not-too-expensive brut Champagne or sparkling wine
2	4	ounces Gorgonzola cheese, *crumbled*
1/2	1	teaspoon freshly ground black pepper, or to taste
2	4	ounces parmesan cheese (ideally, imported Italian Parmesan Reggiano), *grated* (2 ounces = 1/2 cup)
1	2	bunch(es) of chives, *diced* or, green part of 2* green onions, *minced* (for garnish)

1 Heat the oil in a stockpot over medium heat, then add garlic and leek. Cook and stir for about 6 minutes, or until the leek is translucent.

2 Add the rice and stir thoroughly for 2 minutes, making sure that all of the rice grains are lightly coated in oil.

3 Add 1/2 cup* of stock and stir occasionally — or constantly if you don't trust me. (Adjust heat as required for an active simmer.)

4 When the stock is almost all absorbed, add another 1/2 cup* of stock and continue stirring occasionally. Each 1/2 cup* of liquid will take about 5 minutes to be absorbed. Repeat the process 1/2 cup* at a time until 4 cups* of stock have been absorbed.

5 Add the mushrooms and asparagus and continue adding liquid, but from here on, alternate between 1/2 Cup* champagne and 1/2 cup* chicken stock (starting with the Champagne).

6 After adding the last cup of stock, add the gorgonzola and pepper. Stir until the cheese is all melted and the rice is firm, but still creamy.

7 Serve in warm bowls or on warm plates and top with a sprinkle of Parmesan.

le secret Don't be intimidated by all the naysayers.

the adventure club Replace the mushrooms with black truffles, or more of the less expensive white variety. (Instead of adding during cooking, sprinkle fine shavings over the risotto just before serving.)

garnish Sprinkle diced chives or green onion around the perimeter of the plate.

suggested accompaniment Since risotto is very heavy, all accompaniments should be light. Serve with a salad of baby greens and/or glazed baby carrots.

suggested appetizer Sesame-Ginger Broccoli Spears (see page 44).

alternatives i) Risotto, like pasta, works with a wide variety of ingredients and stocks. Add, subtract, or substitute your favorite ingredients. ii) Fresh wild mushrooms may be replaced with rehydrated dried mushrooms. Rehydrate 1 cup* mushrooms by soaking them in 2 cups* boiling water for 30 minutes. Then remove and slice the mushrooms, and reserve the liquid. Add the liquid to the rice in place of an equal amount of stock halfway through cooking.

notes Although risotto does not require constant attention, it cannot be made by an absentee cook. Consequently, this recipe is best made on occasions when it's appropriate for your friends to hang out with you in the kitchen.

guest assignment Stirrer.

hints for advance prep i) Risotto may be cooked 1 hour in advance. To do so, leave out 1 cup *each* of the stock and Champagne, and the Gorgonzola and Parmesan. Before serving, reheat the risotto and add in the remaining liquid and cheese per the original instructions. ii) The vegetables may be prepped in advance and refrigerated in an airtight container.

cooking apparatus One stockpot.   **serving apparatus** Serving plates or bowls.

prep time Fifteen minutes.   **cooking time** About one hour.

music to dine by

1 Fellini/Rota *La Dolca Vita Original Soundtrack* Silva Screens Records Ltd.

2 Mozart *Don Giovanni, Otto Lemperer, Conductor* EMI Classics

3 Frank Sinatra *Sinatra Reprise: The Very Good Years* Reprise

4 Various Artists *MusicalMeals Italian Dinner*
Sony Music Special Products

5 Pavarotti *Puccini's LaBoheme,*
Herbert Von Karajan, Conductor London

wine Chianti Classico

* Double for 12 servings

drunken shrimp creole

This foolproof one-pot recipe borrows its essential elements from the classic Cajun dish.
Shell d'em shrimp and *laissez les bons temps rouler.*

servings

6	12	
1	2	tablespoon(s) olive oil
1-1/2	3	pounds large shrimp, *shelled and deveined.* (SAVE SHELLS FOR STOCK.)
2	4	bay leaves
2	4	celery stalks, *top third, including leafy section cut off, diced, and reserved for stock and, the remainder diced*
1	2	leek(s), thoroughly washed, *top third cut off, diced, and reserved for stock, the remainder diced*
1	2	medium-sized cooking onion(s), *diced*
2	4	teaspoons fresh thyme, *remove and discard stems before measuring*
1/4	1/2	cup butter
5	10	garlic cloves, *minced*
1	2	yellow bell pepper(s), *seeds and membranes discarded cut into 1/4 inch pieces*
1/4	1/2	teaspoon freshly ground black pepper
1/4	1/2	teaspoon cayenne pepper
1	2	teaspoon(s) celery salt
6	12	medium tomatoes, *coarsely diced*
1	2	12-ounce bottle(s) dark beer
1	2	tablespoon(s) Worcestershire sauce
2	4	teaspoons Tabasco sauce
2	4	tablespoons freshly squeezed lemon juice

shrimp stock

1 Heat the oil in a stockpot over medium-high heat.

2 Add the reserved shrimp shells and stir for about 1 minute, or until they turn pink. Add 4 cups* of water, bay leaves, celery and leek tops, one fourth of the onion, and half of the thyme.

3 Bring to a boil, then immediately reduce heat to medium-low and simmer, uncovered, for 40 minutes. (Adjust heat as required to simmer.)

4 The liquid should reduce to 1 cup of rich stock. Strain through a strainer or sieve, and discard solids. Set stalk aside. Rinse the pot.

creole

1 Melt the butter over medium-high heat in the same pot. Add the remaining onion, leek, and celery, as well as the garlic and bell pepper(s). Cook, stirring frequently, for 10 minutes.

2 Add the black pepper, celery salt, remaining cayenne and fresh thyme. Cook and stir for 2 more minutes.

3 Add the tomatoes, beer, shrimp stock, Worcestershire, and Tabasco sauce. Increase heat to medium-high, bring to a boil, then immediately reduce heat to medium-low and simmer, uncovered, for 30 minutes. (Adjust heat as required to simmer.)

4 As your guests are heading for the table, add the shrimp and stir for about 3 minutes, or until pink throughout.
5 Stir in the lemon juice and serve.

le secret Do not overcook shrimp.
the adventure club Collect unusual hot sauces on your travels. Place them in the center of the table and let your guests play with fire.
garnish Lemon wedges.
suggested accompaniment Rice and Greens (see page 88).
suggested appetizer Baby Greens salad (see page 60) with toasted pecans.
alternatives The tomatoes may be replaced with 8 cups* (40 ounces*) of canned peeled tomatoes.
notes Despite the fact that I usually advocate using store bought stocks, the homemade shrimp stock provides a flavorful base that is integral to this recipe.
guest assignment Rice maker
hints for advance prep i) The stock may be made up to 3 days in advance, or frozen for up to 6 months. ii) The rest of the dish may be made 2 days in advance. Add shrimp when reheating.
cooking apparatus A stock pot, a sauté pan, and a strainer or sieve.
serving apparatus Dinner plates.
prep time Fifteen minutes
cooking time One hour and 45 minutes.
music to dine by
1 Balfa Bros. *The Balfa Bros. Play Traditional Cajun Music* Swallow Records
2 Clifton Chenier *Zydeco Dynamite; The Clifton Chenier Anthology* Rhino Records
3 Preservation Hall Jazz Band *Best of the Preservation Hall Jazz Band* CBS/Sony
4 Various Artists *MusicalMeals Cajun Cookin'* Sony Music Special Products
5 Various Artists *The Big Easy, Original Soundtrack* Mango/Island
wine Chenin Blanc

* Double for 12 servings

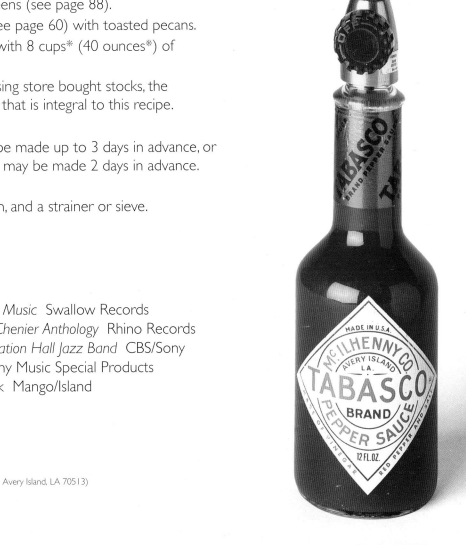

baked salmon with cilantro sauce

The cats in the neighborhood will be your best friends when they see you prepare this catch.

servings

6	12	
		### cilantro sauce
1	2	tablespoon(s) butter
1	2	leek(s), white part only, *finely chopped and thoroughly washed*
1	2	shallot(s), *minced*
1	2	jalapeño chili(es), *seeds and membranes discarded, finely diced*
2	4	garlic cloves, *minced*
1-1/2	3	cups chicken stock (use canned stock or see page 114)
2	4	cups lightly packed fresh cilantro, *remove and discard stems before measuring*
3	6	tablespoons freshly squeezed lime juice
1/4	1/2	teaspoon salt
1/2	1	teaspoon freshly ground black pepper
3	6	tablespoons sour cream
		### salmon
2	4	tablespoons olive oil
6 .	12	6-ounce salmon fillets
6	12	tablespoons freshly squeezed lime juice
		salt and freshly ground black pepper to taste

instructions

cilantro sauce

1 Melt the butter over medium heat in a sauté pan.
2 Add the leek(s), shallot(s), jalapeño chili(es), and garlic and sauté for about 5 minutes, or until the onions are translucent — but not brown.
3 Reduce heat to medium and add the stock. Simmer, uncovered, for 15 minutes. (Adjust heat as required to simmer.) Liquid should reduce by half.
4 Remove from heat and let cool.
5 Transfer to a blender or food processor and add the cilantro, lime juice, salt, and pepper. Puree until smooth.
6 Add the sour cream and "pulse" until mixed. Set aside.

salmon

1 Preheat the oven to 400° F.
2 Cut three* 12-inch squares of aluminum foil.
3 Grease the shiny side of the foil with the oil. Place 2 fillets side by side on foil and fold up the edges to trap the liquid.

4 Pour 1 tablespoon lime juice over each fillet. Season with salt and pepper.

5 Cover each square with a second piece of foil and fold the edges so that the package is airtight. Bake for about 12 minutes, or until the salmon is flaky and cooked throughout.

6 Unrap the salmon.

7 With a spatula, gently lift the salmon onto warmed plates and top with a generous portion of cilantro sauce.

le secret Do not overcook the salmon.

the adventure club Poach the salmon in a dishwasher. I tried it — it really works! (Wrap salmon fillets in aluminum foil with seasonings, per recipe instructions, and seal extra tightly. Place on top rack with all of yesterday's dishes, add dish detergent, and run through the entire wash and dry cycle.)

garnish Cilantro sprigs.

suggested accompaniment Yellow wax beans, steamed and glazed with a lemon butter sauce.

suggested appetizers Vichyssoise with Roasted Garlic (see page 58).

alternatives i) If you're one of those people who hates cilantro and has noticed that I seem to use it everywhere, replace it with half the amount of fresh dill or tarragon. ii) The salmon may be grilled, broiled, or poached. iii) The salmon may be replaced with Chilean sea bass or another firm mild white fish of choice. iv) Sour cream may be replaced with yogurt. v) Chicken stock may be replaced with vegetable stock (for fish-eating vegetarians).

notes Don't forget to save the leftovers for the cats.

guest assignment Fish pouch assembler.

hints for advance prep The cilantro sauce can be made 1 day earlier and refrigerated. (This makes the rest of the preparation a snap.) Heat in a saucepan before serving.

cooking apparatus Aluminum foil, a blender or food processor, and a spatula.

serving apparatus Dinner plates.

prep time Forty-five minutes.

cooking time Fifteen minutes.

music to dine by

1 Zap Mama *Adventures in Afropea 1* Luaka bop/Warner Bros.

2 Various Artists *Trance Planet, Vol 1* Triloka Records

3 Papa Wemba *The Voyager* Earth Beat/Warner Bros.

4 Various Artists *The Indestructible Beat of Soweto* Shanachie

5 Cirque de Soleil *Alegria* RCA/BMG

wine Sancerre (a French Sauvignon Blanc)

* Double for 12 servings

lobstercapecodstyle

Lobster is rarely served at dinner parties because it has a reputation for being pricey. However, in season, lobsters only cost about $10 to $12 each — not much more than a good steak. This beach-style lobster party relies more on presentation than recipe, but it's guaranteed to elevate your status on the lasagna circuit. Begin by forgetting everything you ever learned about good table manners. Then: Tape down your dining room table with several layers of newspaper • Set each place setting with a nut cracker, a lobster pick, or an escargot fork and a small plate • Set out a stack of napkins or a roll of paper towels • Steam the lobsters • Drop the cooked lobsters onto the middle of the table alongside a variety of sauces (see below) • Go for it!

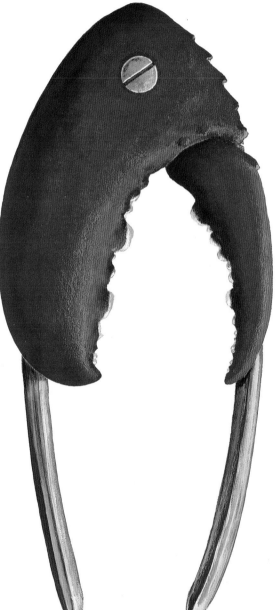

servings

6	12	
		lobster
1	2	teaspoon(s) salt
6	12	Live lobsters, 1-1/4 pounds each (select the liveliest ones)
		lemon-tarragon drawn butter
1/2	1	pound unsalted butter
1/4	1/2	cup fresh tarragon leaves, *finely diced.*
1	2	lemon(s), *zested (see page 113), then juiced*
		ginger-mango puree
1	2	mango(s), *skin and pit discarded, chopped into 1/2 inch cubes*
1/2	1	inch fresh ginger, *peeled and minced*
1/2	1	jalapeño chile, *seeds and membranes discarded, minced*
4	8	fresh basil leaves, *coarsely chopped*
1	2	tablespoon(s) olive oil
1	2	tablespoon(s) seasoned rice vinegar (also known as sushi vinegar)
1/4	1/8	teaspoon salt
		aioli
4	8	garlic cloves, *minced*
1	2	egg yolk(s) at room temperature
1	2	tablespoon(s) freshly squeezed lemon juice
1/8	1/4	teaspoon salt
1	2	cup(s) olive oil
		soy-wasabi dipping sauce
1	2	teaspoon(s) wasabi (Japanese horseradish), *premixed with water*
1/2	1	cup soy sauce (or tamari sauce)

instructions

lobster

1 Add 3 cups of water to a large stockpot with a vegetable steamer. Add the salt and bring to a boil. (A large pot should accommodate up to 6 lobsters. For servings of more than 6, use a second pot.)

2 Drop the live lobsters head first into the pot, cover tightly, and say 10 Hail Marys. Steam for 8 to 10 minutes per pound (12 minutes should be perfect for 1-1/4-pound lobsters).

3 Lobsters will be a deep red color when done. To double check doneness, pull off a walking leg. If it comes away easily, it's done.

4 Remove the lobsters from the pot. Turn each lobster upside down and make a cut through the shell, down the middle of the entire tail. Serve immediately.

lemon-tarragon drawn butter

1 Melt the butter in a heavy saucepan over medium-low heat. When butter is fully melted, remove from heat and let stand for 3 minutes. The butter should settle into three layers: a frothy top, a clear yellow middle, and a milky bottom. Begin by skimming or spooning froth off the top. Then carefully and slowly pour out clear middle layer into a bowl while retaining all of the white sediment in the pan. Discard froth and solids. If necessary, repeat the skimming process on remaining butter in bowl.

2 Add tarragon, lemon zest, and 2 tablespoons* lemon juice to the warm butter. Transfer the butter to a warmed dipping bowl.

ginger-mango purée

1 Puree all the ingredients in a blender or processor until smooth.

aioli

1 Add the garlic, egg yolk(s), lemon juice, and salt to a blender or food processor and purée until smooth. If you do not have a blender or food processor, whisk the ingredients together in a bowl.

2 Slowly pour in the oil with the motor running and purée for about 1 minute, or until the sauce thickens. Cover and refrigerate. If you are using a whisk, keep beating while very gradually adding the oil, until the aioli is thick — this will take several minutes.

soy-wasabi dipping sauce

1 Put the wasabi in a bowl and add 2 tablespoons of the soy sauce.

2 Using the back of a spoon, blend until wasabi is dissolved. Add the remaining soy sauce.

le secret Do not overcook lobster.

the adventure club Make it a BYOL (L is for lobster) party.

garnish If you insist on garnishing everything you eat, tie a bow around each lobster.

suggested accompaniment Bread sticks (see page 52), corn on the cob — both are great with the various dips, tomato wedges, or anything else that can be eaten without utensils.

suggested appetizer This is a very rich dinner. Start with something simple like freshly cut carrot sticks, sans dip.

alternatives Crabs, crayfish, unshelled jumbo shrimp.

notes i) If you are cooking for more than 6, or if your dinner table is large, divide each of the dips into 2 or more bowls. ii) The lemon-tarragon butter and soy-wasabi sauce will separate. Place them in shallow bowls to facilitate a complete dipping experience. iii) To ensure even cooking, select lobsters of similar weight. iv) Dried wasabi (just add water) and seasoned rice vinegar are available in the Asian section of most grocery stores.

guest assignment Running after escaped lobsters.

hints for advance prep Prepare the sauces up to 1 day in advance. (Warm the lemon-tarragon butter just before serving.)

cooking apparatus One very large stockpot, with lid, for every 6 lobsters, and a mini-processor (the ideal tool for making aioli and ginger-mango purée.). **serving apparatus** One lobster cracker, one lobster pick or escargot fork, and one small plate per person, plus a large bowl for shells. **prep time** Forty-five minutes. **cooking time** Fifteen minutes.

music to dine by

1 The Waterboys *Fisherman's Blues* Chrysalis

2 Various Artists, *Hear My Song, Original Soundtrack* Big Screen Music/Giant

3 Van Morrison & The Chieftains *Irish Heartbeat* PolyGram/Mercury

4 Music from the original motion picture soundtrack: *Jaws* MCA

5 Jimmy Buffet *Son of a Sailor* MCA

wine French White Burgundy (ideally, Appellation Chassagne Montrachet)   * Double for 12 servings

thai**coconutcurry**

You don't need to know anything about Thai cooking or curries to make this exotic tasting one-pot meal.
In fact, you don't really even need to know how to cook. Just follow the directions. (*Note:* You do have to know
how to find an Asian grocery store.)

servings

6	12	
2	4	tablespoons toasted sesame oil
3	6	garlic cloves, *minced*
1/2	1	medium cooking onion, *coarsely diced*
1	2	1-inch piece(s) fresh ginger, *peeled and finely diced*
2	4	large carrots, *peeled and sliced into 1/2-inch rounds*
1	2	large potato(es), *peeled and cut into 1/2-inch cubes*
1/2	1	red bell pepper, *seeds and membranes discarded, sliced into 1/8-by-2-inch strips*
1	2	teaspoon(s) ground coriander
1	2	teaspoon(s) ground cardamom
1	2	teaspoon(s) cayenne pepper
4	8	cups vegetable or chicken stock (see page 114)
1	2	14-ounce can(s) coconut milk
3	6	tablespoons freshly squeezed lime juice
2	4	tablespoons of Tom Ka or Tom Yum paste. (Available at any Asian grocery.)
1	2	cup(s) fresh shiitake mushrooms, *stems removed and remainder quartered*
2	4	green onions, *finely sliced*
1	2	cup(s) lightly packed fresh mint, or 1* cup fresh cilantro.
2	4	cups lightly packed spinach leaves. *Remove and discard stems before measuring*

PLUS ONE OF THE FOLLOWING

6	12	
1	2	pound(s) medium shrimp, *shelled and deveined*
1	2	pound(s) boneless chicken thighs or skinless, single breasts, *cut into 1/2-inch cubes*
1	2	pound(s) monkfish or any other firm white fish, *cut into 1/2-inch cubes*
1	2	pound(s) sea scallops
1	2	14-ounce package(s) firm tofu, *cut into 1/2-inch cubes and sautéed in 1 tablespoon vegetable oil + 1 tbsp. toasted sesame oil until brown on all sides*

1 Heat the sesame oil in a stockpot over medium heat and stir in the garlic, onion, and ginger. Stir for 3 minutes.

2 Add the carrots, potato(es), bell pepper, coriander, cardamom, and cayenne. Stir for 2 minutes.

3 Add the stock, coconut milk, lime juice, and Tom Ka or Tom Yum paste. Bring to a boil, reduce heat to medium-low, and simmer, uncovered, for 20 minutes (adjust heat as required to simmer).

4 Add the mushrooms, green onions, and most of the mint or cilantro leaves. (Reserve some for garnish before adding to curry.) Simmer for 5 more minutes.

5 Add the spinach and shrimp, chicken, fish, scallops, or tofu. Cover and simmer for 5 more minutes, or until these additions are cooked through.

6 Serve in warmed shallow bowls. Use an inverted tea cup to mould a round mound of rice in the center of each bowl. Ladle curry around rice.

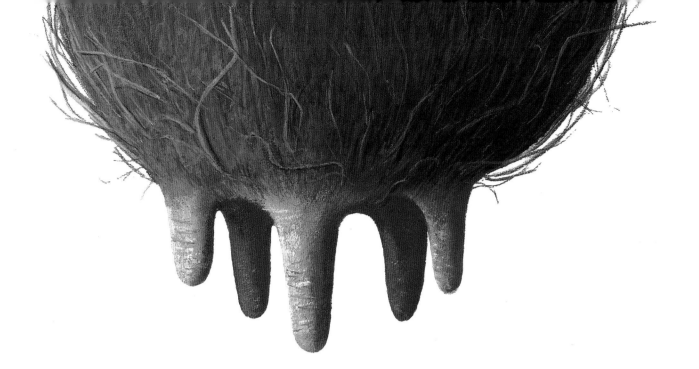

le secret The secret is in the Tom Ka paste (but the details are written in Thai, so it will remain a secret). If you are unable to find the paste, the dish will survive (barely).

the adventure club Add fresh lemongrass. Mince the lower half of 1 stalk, and add it in step 2. Purchase it while you are at the Thai grocery. (While you're there, pick up the coconut milk.)

garnish Sprigs of mint or cilantro.

suggested accompaniment Rice, preferably basmati or jasmine.

suggested appetizer Baby Greens salad (see page 60).

alternatives Add your own favorite veggies. Broccoli spears are a great addition. Add them in step 4

notes Tastes as good, if not better, the next day.

guest assignments Veggie cutter and rice maker.

hints for advance prep This dish may be made 1 day in advance without the shrimp, chicken, or fish. To serve, bring the curry to a boil, add the shrimp, chicken, or fish, and reduce to a hearty simmer for 5 minutes, or until the new ingredients are cooked through.

cooking apparatus One large stockpot.

serving apparatus Individual pasta bowls.

prep time Twenty five minutes.

cooking time Forty minutes.

music to dine by

1 Shoukichi Kina *Asia Classics 2; Peppermint Tea House* Luaka bop/Warner Bros.
2 Ry Cooder & V.M. Baaht *A Meeting by the River* Water Lilly Acoustics
3 Idjah Hadidjah *Tonggeret* Nonsuch/Elektra
4 Various Artists *Royal Court Music of Thailand* Smithsonian Collection Recordings
5 Kid Creole & The Coconuts *Kid Creole Redux* Sire/Warner Bros.

wine Alsatian Gewürztraminer

* Double for 12 servings

steak**cowboy**style

My great uncle was an honest-to-goodness Argentinian gaucho. He worked on the pampas (Argentinian plains) herding cattle to the sea ports. At night, during their rugged treks, the gauchos would sacrifice one of the steers and roast it on a giant spit over an open-pit BBQ of gathered wood. A fiery sauce was concocted in true Argentinian style to spice up the meat. As the outer portion of the meat cooked, it was carved off and devoured by the hungry herders.

The following adaptation of the traditional grilling method has been handed down to me over three generations. It's perfect for informal BBQ parties because it is interactive, requires virtually no setup, and every bit delivers hot, fresh-from-the-grill sizzle. The cayenne-based sauce that the gauchos used is now bottled by my father. For authentic results, order it by mail (see page 116 for address), or simply follow the serving style, substitute your favorite steak sauce, and brand it "an American cowboy cookout."

servings

6	12	
3	6	pounds sirloin steak, 1-1/2 inches thick (ideally, one large steak — ask your butcher)
1/4	1/2	cup of Gaucho Jack's Legendary Argentinian Pepper Sauce, or your favorite steak sauce
2	4	French baguettes, *sliced into 1/2-inch-thick slices*

1 Place the steak on a grill over a hot fire, baste with the sauce and grill until the outer portion reaches the desired degree of doneness.

2 Remove the steak from the grill and slice long strips from the outer edges of the steak. Instruct guests to pick up a steak slice from the cutting board with their fingers, place it on a slice of baguette, and enjoy.

3 Return the remaining steak to the grill, baste, and grill until more of the steak is cooked. Remove and repeat the slicing and serving procedure until steak is consumed.

le secret The secret is in the sauce.

the adventure club Live like a real gaucho.

garnish None required, since the steak never makes it to a plate.

suggested accompaniment Mixed green salad.

suggested appetizer Citrus-Marinated Olives (see page 50)

alternatives i) In a pinch (or a blizzard) steaks may be broiled in an oven. ii) The same grilling and serving method may be used with marinated flank steak.

notes My father made me include this recipe.

guest assignment Steak carver.

hints for advance prep No advance prep is required.

cooking apparatus BBQ, cutting board.

serving apparatus Cocktail napkins.

prep time Five minutes (not counting the time it takes to get the sauce through the mail).

cooking time Fifteen minutes.

music to dine by

1 Astor Piazzolla *Tango Zero Hour* American Clave (Import)
2 Ian Tyson *Cowboyography* Stoney Plain/Vanguard
3 Ennio Morricone *The Legendary Italian Westerns* BMG/RCA
4 Various Artists *Songs of the West, boxed set, Disc 1* Rhino Records
5 Lyle Lovett *Lyle Lovett* Curb/MCA
wine Chilean Cabernet Sauvignon

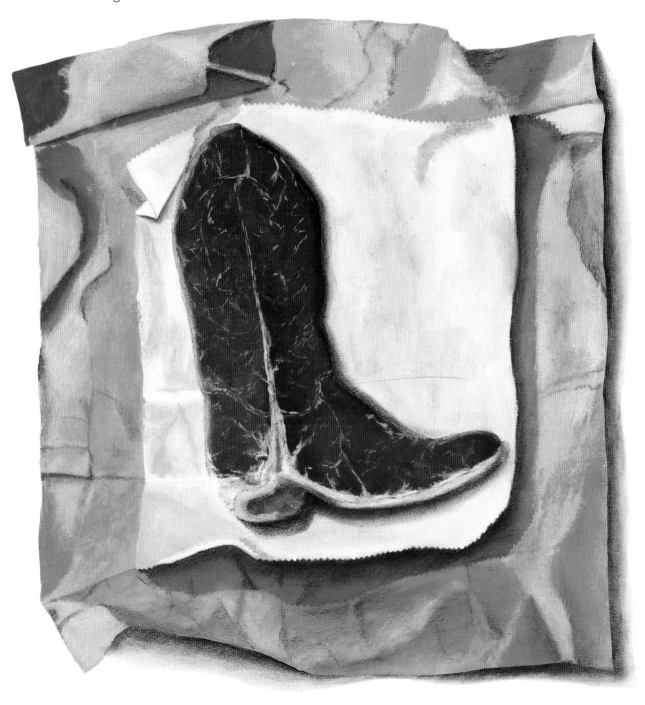

sweet potato stars

A star is born. One or two of these unbelievably simple-to-make stars will add a magical touch to any chicken, fish, or meat entree — or serve a few as a great meat replacement for vegetarians.

servings

6	12	
4	8	large sweet potatoes or yams, at least 3 inches in diameter (should yield 2 stars per person, depending on size)
2	4	tablespoons toasted sesame oil
1	2	cup(s) freshly squeezed orange juice
1-1/2	3	tablespoons brown sugar
1/2	1	teaspoon ground nutmeg
1	2	orange(s), *zested* — after zesting, orange may be juiced (see page 113)

1 Preheat the oven to 350° F.

2 Place each sweet potato or yam on its side and slice crosswise into 1/2-inch rounds.

3 Using a 3-inch star-shaped cookie cutter, cut out a star shape from each round; discard the scraps. If your star cookie cutter is packed away with the Christmas decorations, place a paper star stencil on top of the round and use a paring knife to cut the shape (see page 113 for stencil and illustration).

4 Pour the sesame oil into the bottom of a shallow ovenproof baking dish and spread it so that the whole bottom is greased.

5 Place the stars in the baking dish.

6 Pour the orange juice over the stars and sprinkle the brown sugar and nutmeg on top.

7 Cover tightly with aluminum foil.

8 Bake for 30 minutes, then remove foil and bake for 15 more minutes.

9 Use a spatula to remove the stars from the baking dish. Top each star with 1 teaspoon of the pan juice.

le secret Select large, fat, symmetrical sweet potatoes in order to have the most surface from which to cut the stars. If you are cutting the stars by hand, fear not. Imperfectly shaped stars will be interpreted as a fond reference to *Le Petit Prince*, not a lack of artistry.

the adventure club Create your own shapes.

garnish Grated orange zest on top, and, especially around, stars.

alternatives Cut stars from regular baking potatoes. It's not as exciting but it works nicely and adds an artistic touch to any meat dish. Grease the bottom of the baking dish with olive oil and sprinkle the potato stars with salt, pepper, and fresh or dried rosemary. Drizzle olive oil over the stars.

notes i) When cooking for large groups, you may choose to serve 1 star only on each plate. This is perfectly adequate. ii) There is no need to peel the potatoes because all of the skin is removed when the star shape is cut.

guest assignment Star cutter.

hints for advance prep Cut the stars up to 1 day in advance and keep them refrigerated in water to preserve their freshness and color.

cooking apparatus One three-inch star-shaped cookie cutter (optional), available at most cookingware stores for about a dollar; an ovenproof baking dish, preferably glass (a 9-by-12-inch dish holds about 12 stars); and aluminum foil.

prep time About 20 minutes, depending on your star-cutting speed. A star-shaped cookie cutter cuts the prep time in half.

cooking time 45 minutes.

88Ⓐ
The Tuber
Agency

SWEETIE

To Bob,
Best wishes,
♡ Love, Sweetie

PHOTO: Dick Kaiser

© Tuber Agency. Permission to reproduce limited to editorial uses only.

greens

This is a basic greens recipe. There is nothing particularly Surreal about it. I've included it as a reminder that greens are tasty, nutritious, underutilized in most kitchens, and a perfect addition to any contemporary meal.

servings

6	12	
3	6	pounds of mustard greens, kale, Swiss chard, turnip or beet tops, collard greens or spinach, or a mixture, *washed thoroughly, but not dried, thick stems and mid-ribs removed*
2	4	tablespoons olive oil
4	8	garlic cloves, minced
1	2	tablespoon(s) freshly squeezed lemon juice
1	2	teaspoon(s) balsamic vinegar (optional)
1/8	1/4	teaspoon salt
1/3	2/3	teaspoon freshly ground black pepper

1 Add the wet greens to a large pot over medium-high heat and cook them in their own moisture for about 5 minutes, or until wilted. Keep covered, stirring occasionally. (Greens for 12 will require a few extra minutes.)

2 Remove the greens from the pot, drain off any excess water, and chop them coarsely.

3 Add the oil and garlic to a sauté pan over medium heat and cook for about 2 minutes, or until garlic just begins to brown. Add the greens and sauté for 3 more minutes.

4 Add the lemon juice, vinegar, salt, pepper and any Adventure Club toppings. Toss and serve immediately.

le secret Fresh crisp greens.

the adventure club Top with shavings of imported Italian Parmesan cheese, 1 tablespoon* walnut or toasted sesame oil, and/or toasted nuts.

garnish Lemon slices.

alternatives Follow the same procedure using spinach only.

notes Remind yourself to eat greens more often.

guest assignment Greens washer.

hints for advance prep The greens may be washed and stemmed 1 day in advance. Cover and keep refrigerated.

cooking apparatus A large pot and a sauté pan

prep time Ten minutes.

cooking time Fifteen minutes.

* Double for 12 servings

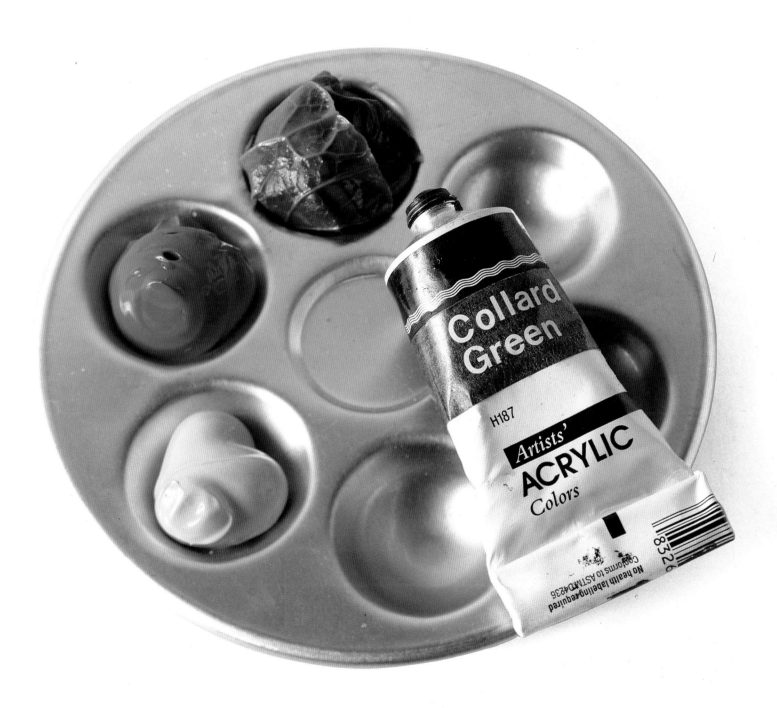

10 more*ways to avoid making dessert

Chances are you will have seen all you want to of your kitchen by the time dessert rolls around.
If your guests haven't lavished you with homemade brownies or other delectable treats,
whip out one of the following instantaneous crowd pleasers:

1 Frozen Ice Cream Treats
Old School: Fudgsicles, Orangsicles, or Popsicles
New School: Häagen Dazs, Ben & Jerry's, or Dove bars.
The Adventure Club: Flag down an ice cream truck and buy pop-ups, rockets, chocolate éclairs, etc.

2 Fortune Cookies
The Adventure Club: Pull out the fortunes with tweezers and replace them with your own prophecies.

3 Chocolate-covered Espresso Beans
A low-fuss mocha latte.

4 Oreos & Milk
Bound to trigger fond childhood memories.

5 Chocolate Truffles
Not a calorie in sight!

6 Frozen Dough Cookies
Serve hot out of the oven.
The Adventure Club: Pretend they are homemade and see if you can get away with it.

7 An Assortment of Penny Candy
(See "The Treasure Chest," page 18)

8 Pepperidge Farm Pirouettes & Freshly Brewed Coffee
The Adventure Club: Serve flavored coffee (i.e., vanilla, hazelnut, almond, etc.)

9 Chocolate Fondue
Melt chocolate bars, whisk in a splash of milk, and dip in fresh fruit. Serve (ideally) in a fondue pot or in a heated bowl.

10 Play spin-the-bottle instead

* For the original 10 Ways to Avoid Making Dessert, see *The Surreal Gourmet: Real Food for Pretend Chefs*.

creative cocktails

fruit-infused cordials

If you've ever been to a bar and seen a giant jar of fruit stewing, chances are they are making infused alcohol. It's simple to make, exotic looking, and provides a variety of serving options. It takes a few days to steep, so you must be patient.

FILL A 2-QUART (OR 2-LITER) GLASS JAR WITH SEVERAL OR ALL OF THE FOLLOWING:

1/2 pineapple, *sliced. Skin and core discarded*
1 cup strawberries, *halved. Stems discarded*
1 cup blackberries
1 peach, *sliced. Skin and pit discarded*
1 mango, *sliced. Skin and pit discarded*
1 orange, *sections separated. Peel discarded.*
1 banana, *peeled and sliced*

1 Add one 25-ounce bottle of tequila, vodka, gin or golden rum. Cover tightly and let stand at room temperature for at least 3 days, and preferably 1 week.

2 Strain or serve directly from the jar ("sun tea" jars come with handy spigots). Serve chilled in shot glasses, or over ice with or without sparkling mineral water.

3 The "pickled" fruit may be blended with ice for an instant frozen daiquiri or Margarita — especially delicious when made from rum- or tequila-soaked fruit.

Note: Best when made with very ripe fruit.

pimm's no.1 cup

Pimm's is a staple British summer drink. It is best described as a gin-based version of sangría.
Mix a pitcherful and toast the Queen.

servings

6	12	
1	2	lime(s), *sliced*
1	2	orange(s), *sliced*
1	2	cucumber(s), *peeled and sliced*
1	2	handful(s) fresh strawberries, *stems removed*
12	24	fresh mint sprigs
6	12	ounces Pimm's No. 1 Cup
24	48	ounces lemon-flavored soda (7-up, Sprite, etc.)
12	24	ounces sparkling mineral water (or club soda)

1 Place the lime(s), orange(s), cucumber(s), strawberries, and half of the mint in the bottom of a glass pitcher.** Add the Pimm's and 6 ounces* of the lemon-flavored soda. Let stand for 30 minutes.

2 Add the remaining lemon-flavored soda and the mineral water. Stir and serve over ice.

3 Top each glass with cucumber, lime, and orange slices and strawberries from the pitcher, and garnish with mint sprig.

frozen vodka

If you are planning on serving cocktails and you enjoyed arts and crafts in elementary school, here's a little trick to impress the vodka drinkers. Take a half-gallon cardboard milk or juice carton. Empty and rinse it. Unfold the top so that it has only 4 sides (and a bottom). Place a 25-ounce bottle of vodka inside the carton. Add decorations between the bottle and the carton walls. To be thematic, use lemon, lime, and orange slices for lemon vodka, hot peppers for pepper vodka, etc. Or create your own theme with plastic toys, flowers, penny candies, etc. Fill the carton with water. (*Note:* the purer the water, the clearer the ice.) Place your work of art, standing upright, in the freezer overnight. Before the party, cut and peel away the milk carton. Set your "ice sculpture" on a plate and encourage guests to serve themselves.

mulled wine

The perfect method for thawing out guests when they arrive on a cold winter's night.

servings

6	12	
1	2	teaspoon(s) whole cloves or 2* cinnamon sticks
1	2	teaspoon(s) aniseed
1/2	1	cup freshly squeezed orange juice
2	4	tablespoons honey
1/2	1	cup Calvados or Southern Comfort
1	2	orange(s) sliced
1	2	bottle(s) of Cabernet Sauvignon or other dry red wine

1 Combine all the ingredients in a large saucepan. Gently simmer over medium heat for 30 minutes.
2 Pour through a strainer. Save orange slices and discard remaining solids.
3 Pour the wine into heated mugs. Add 1 orange slice per mug and serve.

* Double for 12 servings
** 12 serving will require 2 pitchers

partytime

surreal party etiquette

For many guests, dinner parties are daunting affairs. Common party phobias include a fear of arriving too early — or too late — being dressed inappropriately, forgetting names, and drinking too much. It's courteous to anticipate these potential scenarios, and preempt any dramas *du soir*.

introductions Some people dream of inventing a word that is added to Webster's dictionary. My dream is to eliminate the following form of introduction: "Do you two know each other?" As you might guess, the other person invariably says yes just as I am saying no. "Do you know me?" and "Do you remember my name?" should also be outlawed. Instead of embarrassing your guests, risk being redundant by introducing them to one another as though for the first time. Before ducking out, help to establish a conversational flow. Break the ice by incorporating common ground into your introduction (i.e., children, work, places they've lived, etc.).

It's a fact: Martians have stolen our short-term memories. Help save face for your intergalactic victims by continuously weaving guests' names into the conversation.

the art of seating Who is seated by whom can stimulate conversation and enrich the natural energy of the evening. A little policing is usually required. Keep the silent types out of the far corners, and away from the ringer (to avoid their being trampled). Split up couples and good friends who may get too insular, and pair those who have the potential to complement — and hopefully to compliment — one another. If you have a seating plan in mind and don't want your guests to deviate, put a place card at each setting. If place cards seem too formal, spell out the names or initials with alphabet cereal or letters clipped from a newspaper. If you want to avoid place cards altogether, do it subtlely ("Quincy, why don't you sit here . . ."). For a change of pace, ignore the conventional boy/girl, boy/girl tradition.

the smoking issue Decide in advance where you would like smokers to smoke — i.e., anywhere, in just one room, or only outside. Placing ashtrays in the designated areas is a subtle signal that most smokers are accustomed to looking for. If the only suitable option is outside, make your guests feel comfortable, not ostracized. The longer they are out in the cold (figuratively, if not literally) the more time they will have to do that smoker's bonding thing — which invariably leads to dredging up stories about your checkered past.

jobs that make guests feel useful

- greeter/coat hanger
- mingler/introducer
- car key DWI czar
- tour guide
- bartender
- dj
- finger food server
- sous-chef
- grillmeister
- photographer/videographer

the drinking issue There are two types of people who require extra attention at a party: those who don't drink and those who drink too much. Nondrinkers usually fall into three categories; teetotalers who have never fancied drinking, pregnant women, and "reformed" drinkers who used to drink too much and now don't drink at all. For some members of the latter group, abstinence is no picnic. Being surrounded by a group of revelers who get collectively looser and more boisterous can compound the abstainers' discomfort and turn a seemingly fun time into an unpleasant experience. Some of this is inevitable, but you can reduce the discomfort level by: **a)** not drawing attention to non-drinkers; **b)** stocking a full complement of nonalcoholic beverages (see page 21); **c)** serving these in the same glasses you are using for cocktails and wine; and **d)** offering to brew a fresh pot of coffee or tea at any time without making it seem like a bother.

Heavy drinkers fall into categories as well — usually face first. Most adults do not appreciate being "cut off," especially when they are in mid-flight. It's best to recognize the problem before it's too late. A discreet friend-to-friend conversation is generally your best course of action.

My own exhaustive morning-after research has determined that toward the end of the evening, people tend to continue drinking as a reflex action rather than from a desire to consume more alcohol. Present a second option by putting out bottles of sparkling mineral water. If you are serving mixed drinks, drastically reduce the amount of alcohol you pour for each drink. Your guests will thank you in the morning.

the drug issue If you think President Clinton only took one puff and didn't inhale, I have two words for you: *spin control*. The reality is that many responsible, otherwise law-abiding adults are forced into the closet by the laws and stigmas attached to smoking marijuana. As with the cigarette smoking issue, decide in advance what your response will be. If it is yes, designate an appropriate area — you'll be amazed at who partakes once the ice is broken. If you feel uncomfortable, for whatever reason, don't succumb to peer pressure. Just say no.

Treat smokers with the same care as drinkers and do not let anyone drive away under the influence.

the great escape Here's a nifty trick for the next time you find yourself held captive at your own party in an extended one-on-one conversation with no polite avenue of escape. It was taught to me by a savvy band tour manager who claims it is used by the Queen of England. As is the case for most escape artist tricks, an accomplice is required.

Before the party, establish a distress signal with your accomplice. It should be something very simple (i.e., tugging your right earlobe), but not something you do unconsciously. If you find yourself cornered during the party, catch your accomplice's eye and tug your earlobe, signaling an immediate need to be called away due to "an impending culinary disaster." My advice is, keep it subtle — or you will look like a third base coach giving the bunt signal.

party games

- twister (do not play immediately following a large meal)
- charades
- pictionary
- trivial pursuit I, II or III
- karaoke (a special sound system is required)
- scruples
- balderdash
- musical pears (see page 109)
- the dictionary game
- guess who
- write the opening to a short story and have each guest add a paragraph

theartofflexibility

One of my mentors, the president of a major record label, was in the midst of a raging business crisis. Over lunch, I asked how he was coping. "I can't angst over it," he responded. "Cancer is bad, AIDS is bad, a brain tumor is bad. This is nothing."

Although something is always bound to go wrong at a party, with the exception of mass food poisoning and/or choking, no catastrophe merits spoiling the evening.

Be prepared. But if that doesn't work, be prepared to wing it.

too much, too little, too late   If you run out of food, booze, or ice, call a restaurant or store that delivers. If that's not an option, try borrowing from an accommodating neighbor (knock on his or her door with a piece of dessert in hand). If neither the store nor your neighbor delivers, order the goods with a credit card and call a taxi to pick them up.

When only half the anticipated guests show up, and you are resigned to the fact that no one else is going to arrive, reconfigure everything to suit the number of people in attendance. Remove excess settings and chairs, fold up the table flaps, and reduce the volume of food accordingly. If no one, or nearly no one, shows up, look out the window for signs of imminent natural disasters. If none are in sight, check the date in your daybook. If it's the correct day, ask yourself: "Am I a bad person?" If the answer is no, divide the dinner up into single portions, freeze them, and mix yourself a Martini.

If twice as many people show up, consider yourself a social and culinary god and mix yourself a Martini to celebrate. Halve all portions, double the garnish, and rechristen the meal California cuisine. The freeloaders will be so grateful to be welcomed at such a popular event that they will never notice the difference.

so sous me   There's someone at every dinner party who sneaks into the kitchen, sticks a spoon into each pot, samples the fare, and starts making comments about what he or she would do to improve the flavor. If his or her help is a welcome reprieve, lasso that person with an apron before they change their mind. If everything's under control, ask to see the intruder's Michelin rating or Cordon Bleu cooking school certificate. If no credentials are provided, escort the meddler politely to the kitchen door.

tips for enjoying your own party

- select a menu that can be prepared entirely in advance.
- shop for food, prep it, and clean your home 1 day in advance.
- do not invite anyone for whom you need to remain on your best behavior (i.e., a potential employer or prospective mother-in-law).
- structure the evening into three sections: cooking, socializing, and cleaning up.
- invite friends you want to spend time with into the inner sanctum of your kitchen.
- drink enough — but not too much.
- seat yourself next to your favorite guest.
- switch seats during dinner so that you have a chance to talk to everyone.
- be sure to have someone to conduct a postmortem with after the guests have left.
- hire someone to clean up or, if you have a regular cleaning person, plan for the party the night before he or she is scheduled to clean.

rescue 911 — how to bail out a boring party

- raid your party treasure chest (see page 18).
- phone the white house: (202) 456-1414.
- do the french "switcheroo" (see page 107).
- play truth or dare.
- change the music (see page 100).
- find a polaroid with an autotimer and take group photos.
- put yourself out of your misery and send everyone home.
- put someone else in charge and leave.

LOCAL ALARM.

IN CASE OF ZZZZ
BREAK GLASS

aames security
CORPORATION

records to shift a party into 2nd gear

The B-52's *Cosmic Thing* Reprise
Deee-Lite *World Clique* Elektra
Jerry Lee Lewis *Original Sun Greatest Hits* Rhino
James Brown *Live at the Apollo* Polydor
Bee Gees *Saturday Night Fever* Polydor
Talking Heads *Stop Making Sense* Sire Records
Parliament Funkadelic *Tear the Roof Off (1974-1980)* Casablanca
The Rolling Stones *Hot Rocks (1964-1971)* ABKCO Records
Various Artists *Atlantic Soul Classics* Warner Special Products
Blondie *Best of Blondie* Chrysalis
The Village People *Greatest Hits* Rhino
Elvis Costello *My Aim Is True* Rykodisc
K.C. & the Sunshine Band *The Best of K.C. & the Sunshine Band* Rhino

theparty'sover

"so long, farewell, auf weidersehen, goodbye..."   If you're dreaming about hitting the sack while your guests are hitting the sake, try dropping a hint. Change the music to "Na Na Na Na, Hey Hey, Goodbye" by Steam, or Woody Guthrie's "So Long, It's Been Good to Know You."   If these are not among your collection, a personal atonal rendition can convey the message nicely. If that doesn't work, begin noisily doing the dishes. When all else fails, say goodnight and go to bed.

the clean up   When guests volunteer to clear the table, the offer is usually sincere. When they offer to stick around to clean up and help do the dishes, what they are really saying is: "Wow, that's an awful mess you've got here, but I'm tired and I have an early meeting tomorrow."   Interpret such offers as you wish, but if you let them off the hook, you are paving the way to a guilt-free exit from their next soiree.

   How much *you* are capable of tackling after the last guest departs depends on the capacity of your reserve-energy bank. Nothing can make cleaning up fun, but singing along to a favorite oldie at top volume (try The Monkeys, *Missing Links*, Rhino Records) is sure to help generate a second wind. If you need motivation, and don't mind treating yourself like a trained seal, save a piece of something delectable (preferably chocolate) as your little reward for completing the task.

the postmortem   It always adds to the fun if a spouse, lover, or confidante hangs around to conduct a party "postmortem" after the guests have gone. Even the worst culinary crises, political gaffs, and social faux pas can be laughed at when scrutinized under the postmortem microscope. Bad hair, bad dress, bad manners, and bad dates are all fair game once the guests are safely on their way. If this seems uncharitable, don't fret: they're sure to be critiquing you and your party on the drive home. I love to pull up a stool by the sink, sit my co-conspirator down beside me, and let fly while I clean. It's actually possible to plow through an entire stack of dishes while losing yourself in the excitement of such gossip.

how to keep inebriated guests from driving home

**Above all, at every step, make your guests feel
good about their decision not to drive.**

- **Collect keys at the door as guests enter.**
- **Create a cab fee insurance fund (i.e., everyone contributes
  two dollars as they enter).**
- **Pre-designate drivers.**
- **Provide a comfortable sleeping space and promise an enticing
  breakfast and lots of aspirin.**
- **Post the number of a safe-ride service or a friendly taxi company.**
- **Ride share: Match those who need rides with those who can drive.**
- **Body tackle.**

the
advanced
adventure
club

Planning, shopping, and cooking for a conventional dinner party is a challenge in itself for anyone who has an actual life. Nonetheless, for the culinary loose cannons among you, on those rare occasions when my Adventure Club suggestions still leave you searching for some higher peak to scale, when time is on your side, and you want to pull out all the stops, I offer inspiration and suggestions in the form of the Advanced Adventure Club. Initially, the following concepts existed solely as fantasies. But when I actually tested the meals on my unsuspecting friends, I discovered that preparing the various components was a bit like setting up an elaborate magic trick. Somewhere in the complex process of constructing these culinary capers, I found I experienced what can only be described as a natural cook's high. Of course, it may have been the garlic…

the all-Elvis evening

Cook a meal fit for the King. Buy one of the cookbooks such as *Are You Hungry Tonight* (see page 116) featuring Elvis's favorite recipes, and create your own Elvis feast (you may want to reduce the portion sizes). Play Elvis music and videos all night, and to be fully authentic, wheel the TV set up to the dining room table and leave it on during dinner. (I learned this bit of Elvis trivia on my tour of Graceland.) If this isn't adventurous enough, have *everyone* dress up as Elvis, hire an Elvis impersonator, or rent a Karaoke machine and let your guests interpret their favorite Elvis classics.

note Those of you who scoff at the idea of Elvis cuisine may be surprised to discover that the King's favorite foods included some healthy southern delicacies such as collard greens, baked sweet potatoes and black-eyed peas. Whether you choose to create a "thin Elvis" or a "fat Elvis" dinner, don't resist the temptation to serve fried peanut butter and banana sandwiches as an appetizer, and Twinkies for dessert.

music to shake your hips by Elvis Presley *50,000,000 Elvis Fans Can't Be Wrong* RCA

wine Elvis never drank alcohol, but he consumed Pepsi and orange soda by the truckload.

monocuisine

Prepare an entire meal made with ingredients of the same color, or the same two colors. If you are stuck for ingredients or inspiration, exercise poetic license and add colored namesakes like red snapper, Black Forest cake, or duck a l'orange to the mix.

Do not divulge the menu and keep everyone out of the kitchen. Let guests pick up on the theme at their own speed. Be a little playful and drop subtle hints (i.e., serve something incongruous like cheese puffs before an orange dinner, or use flowers and napkins that match your color of choice).

Here are a few color suggestions:

white

White Russians
Vichyssoise
Cauliflower
White asparagus
White bean salad
Garlic mashed potatoes
Chilean sea bass
White chocolate mousse
wine Sauvignon Blanc
music The Beatles,
The White Album, Capitol/EMI

yellow

Banana daiquiris
Corn chowder
Saffron rice
Yellow curry chicken
Yellow bell peppers
Lemon pie
wine Chardonnay
music Yellow Man, *Yellow Man Rides Again*, RAS Records

black

Black Russians
Black caviar
Black bean soup
Pumpernickel bread
Squid ink pasta with
"Blackened" chicken
dark chocolate mousse
wine Black Tower
music Prince: *The Black Album,* Warner Bros.

orange

Vodka and orange juice
Smoked salmon appetizers
Cheddar cheese sticks
Carrot sticks
Carrot or pumpkin soup
Sweet potato stars (page 86)
Stuffed orange bell peppers
Kumquats
Orange sherbet
wine ??
music XTC, *Oranges and Lemons*, Geffen

pink

Vodka and pink grapefruit juice
Cream of tomato soup
Poached salmon
Rose potatoes
Strawberry ice cream
wine Pink Champagne
music The Band, *Music from the Big Pink,* Capital/EMI

red

Bloody Marys
Roasted red bell pepper soup (see page 56)
Red pasta with tomato sauce beet risotto
Baked tomatoes
Raspberry sorbet
wine Claret
music Simply Red, *Stars*, East West America

thesurrealmeal

Prepare a truly Surreal meal, where all the food is made from one set of ingredients, but presented to look like foods from other food groups. In the heyday of Surrealism back in the thirties and forties, Salvador Dalí threw lavish parties where he melded food and decor into a new medium of creative expression. The photographs below are taken from a dinner that I created for an evening sponsored by the Salvador Dalí Museum in St. Petersburg, Florida. Let your mind run wild or mimic this meal by going to your local art supply store, buying painter's palettes ($4 each), and arranging any assortment of brightly colored puréed seasoned vegetables with a filet of chicken, fish, or beef.

music to dine by Tom Waits/Crystal Gayle *One from the Heart, Original Soundtrack* Columbia
wine Le Cigare Volant, Bonny Doon Vineyards

Assorted, Highly Spiced, puréed vegetables with a baked Salmon Fillet

Ice Cream eggs with sorbet Yolks

Black olive Paste

french dressing

(Not a meal suggestion…but definitely an adventure). When I was researching this book, several of my friends informed me of a French (some say British) dinner party tradition. Apparently, at midnight couples discreetly leave the room, trade clothes with each other, and return to the party. Now, I'm a pretty liberal guy, but cross-dressing is not prominent among my list of fantasies. Nonetheless, for those of you who have "done it all," I am assured that this makes for some pretty interesting conversation — and is guaranteed to pull a boring party out of the doldrums.

music to switch by   Various artists, *The Crying Game (Featuring Boy George)*, SBK Records, and/or Original London Cast Soundtrack: *The Rocky Horror Picture Show,* First Night Records.

wine   Chances are you have had enough wine already.

thefrozenTV dinnerswitcheroo

In this culinary ruse, your guests are fooled by a home-cooked meal served in a store-bought aluminum frozen TV dinner container.

Start by purchasing low-end TV dinners (one per guest — all the same kind). Empty the contents (feed them to kids, or repack and refreeze them) and replace them with gourmet look-alikes (i.e., substitute frozen mashed potatoes with freshly whipped roasted garlic mashed potatoes). Pore through some cookbooks to find recipes that match the look of the original food you are replacing. Or, take a shortcut and purchase prepared foods at a gourmet store.

Stuff the replacement dinner (in its tray) back in the original cardboard box, and serve the box intact. Technically, no one would reheat the frozen dinner in the box, but this allows your guests to compare your meal to the photograph on the cover.

A little thespian posturing is required at showtime. Before presenting the faux TV dinners, explain that you encountered a mini-emergency and you had no time to prepare the intended meal. Claim that you thought of canceling the party but instead opted to let the show go on. Look desperate and apologetic, then serve the dinners and watch your guests' faces.

If you are fearful that no one will notice the difference between your food and a frozen dinner, cook up a variation on the theme by revealing the joke before the food is consumed (i.e., serve a frozen fish sticks dinner that when uncovered reveals a beautiful piece of salmon).

music to switch channels by Various Artists, *The TV Theme Song Sing-Along Album*, Rhino Records

wine Serve any wine that is appropriate for the meal your guests expect to be served.

★ ★ ★ ★ ★ musical pears ★ ★ ★ ★ ★

(A Surreal game of charades)

Each name on this list represents a band or solo artist who shares their/his/her name with a food. Some of the names are a bit of a stretch — but hey, that's rock n' roll. (Hint: Remember that different cultures eat different foods.) Xerox this page, cut the names up, and place them in a hat. Conventional charades rules apply.

Adam Ant	Chick Corea	Humble Pie	Pearl Jam
April Wine	Chicken Shack	The Jam	Phish
Mark Almond	The Chiffons	Ice T	Pigpen
A Taste of Honey	Chilliwack	Ice Cube	Robert Plant
Bad Brains	Chocolate Jam Company	Jelly	Iggy Pop
B52s	Chocolate Milk	Jellybread	Popcorn
Ginger Baker	Colt 45	Joy of Cooking	Potatoes
Bananarama	Ry Cooder	Kid Creole and the Coconuts	Rabbit
Banana Splits	Counting Crows	Kingfish	Raspberries
The Beatles	Country Joe and the Fish	Lemonheads	Red Hot Chili Peppers
Beaverteeth	Cracker	Lemon Pipers	Ruben and the Jets
Belly	The Cranberries	Lemmon Sisters	Rice and Beans Orchestra
The Beat Farmers	Cream	Lime Spiders	Roosters
Jellybean Benitez	Tim Curry	Limelighters	Rosemary Clooney
Chuck Berry	Dixie Cups	Little Caesar	Salt-N-Pepa
Heidi Berry	Ducks Deluxe	Lovin' Spoonful	Sherbet
Bill and Taffy	The Eagles	Lydia Lunch	The Sharks
Blackberries	Eddie Rabbit	Frankie Lymon	Jane Siberry
Black Crowes	Echo and the Bunnyman	Manhattan Transfer	Silver Apples
Blancmange	Electric Prunes	Marmalade	Smashing Pumpkins
Blind Lemon Jefferson	Fine Young Cannibals	Martha and the Muffins	Soup Dragons
Blind Melon	Fishbone	Meat Loaf	Southern Comfort
BLT	Flying Burrito Brothers	Meat Puppets	Strawberry Alarm Clock
Blue Oyster Cult	Ginger	John Mellencamp	Sugar
Bootsauce	Glass Tiger	Midnight Oil	Sugarcubes
Bread	Grapefruit	Mighty Lemon Drops	Sugar Pie DeSanto
Bucks Fizz	Grapes of Wrath	Christopher Milk	Sweet Honey in the Rock
Buckwheat Zydeco	The Gravelberries	Milli Vanilli	Tangerine Dream
Buffalo Springfield	Guyana Kool-Aid	Moby Grape	Turtles
Jimmy Buffett	Hall and Oates	Mom's Apple Pie	Vanilla Fudge
T-Bone Burnett	Hard Meat	Jellyroll Morton	Vanilla Ice
Paul Butterfield	Heart	New Potato Caboose	T-Bone Walker
The Byrds	Henry Cow	Juice Newton	Waterboys
Cake	Herb Alpert	Northern Pikes	Roger Waters
Candy	Buddy Holly and the Crickets	Nutmegs	Muddy Waters
Captain Beefheart	Honeycombs	Olive Lawn	Whitesnake
Catfish	Honeydrippers	Partridge Family	Wild Cherry
Don Cherry	Hot Chocolate	Peanut Butter Conspiracy	Paul McCartney and Wings
Neneh Cherry	Hot Dogs	Elvis Parsley (sorry)	Wishbone Ash
Cherry Vanilla	Hot Tuna	Peaches and Cream	Yardbirds
Mark Chestnut	The Hopping Penguins	Peaches and Herb	Neil Young and Crazy Horse

basics

the**danger**zones
chicken

Poultry is particularly susceptible to contamination by salmonella bacteria, which can cause serious food poisoning (and ruin your cachet on the dinner party circuit). To avoid any problems, follow these rules:

- After handling raw chicken, wash your hands, utensils, and cutting surfaces with soap and hot water to keep any bacteria from spreading to other foods. It is a good habit to cut poultry on a disposable surface such as waxed paper to avoid any contact with cutting boards — a favorite hangout for bacteria.
- Make sure that chicken is always properly refrigerated. Cook fresh chicken within 2 days of purchasing and frozen chicken (kept frozen) within 4 months. Frozen chicken must be fully thawed, preferably in the refrigerator, before cooking. Never take chances. If there is ever a hint that chicken has not been carefully stored (use the good old "smell test"), discard it.
- Cooking and grilling times vary according to the oven or grill temperature and the portion size. Make a small incision in the middle of the chicken to make sure that it is cooked throughout. If any pink remains, continue cooking.
- To be safe, always marinate chicken in the refrigerator.
- After cooking, do not return chicken to the same plate that it was on prior to cooking, and avoid any contact between the cooked chicken and the raw juices.

pork

- To ensure against bacteria, cook all forms of pork thoroughly until the juices run clear. If you have a meat thermometer, 160°F degrees is perfect.

general meat-handling tips

- Meats and poultry are most susceptible to bacteria when exposed to temperatures between 50° and 70° F. Keep all such foods refrigerated until ready for cooking.
- Always store uncooked meats in your refrigerator on a level below other foods, so that their raw juices do not drip onto anything.

coddling eggs

There is a new school of thought that claims eggs should never be consumed unless they are fully cooked throughout. More moderate thinkers believe that coddling an egg will kill most of its potentially harmful bacteria. When I am alone I don't worry about it, but when I'm cooking for groups of people, the fear of a class-action lawsuit drives me to coddle, as follows:

Place the eggs, in their shells, in boiling water for 40 seconds. Remove, run under cold water for 15 seconds to stop the cooking process, and use as directed.

indoor charcoal grilling

Burning charcoal emits carbon monoxide. Proper ventilation is required to disperse the toxic fumes. Only grill indoors under a well-ventilated chimney, and never go to sleep with the coals still burning.

edible flowers

Flowers make beautiful garnishes. However, only certain varieties may be eaten. To be certain that you are not eating poisonous flowers, or flowers that have been treated with pesticides, use store bought edible flowers, or grow your own organic flowers such as violas, pansies, or nasturtiums.

cooking techniques

toasting nuts

pan method Over medium heat, melt 1 teaspoon of butter for every 1/2 cup of nuts. Add the nuts to pan and stir occasionally until browned. Remove the excess butter by drying the nuts on a paper towel.

oven/toaster oven method No fats required. Place the desired amount of nuts on a piece of aluminum foil. Bake in a preheated 350° F oven for about 8 minutes, or until brown, turning them once.

zesting

Make grated lime, lemon, or orange zest by grating the outermost, colored layer of the citrus peel on the fine part of a grater. To protect yourself from pesticide residue, be sure to wash the skin thoroughly before zesting.

chicken tendon removal

To remove the white tendon that runs inside the small fillet of the breast, grasp the top end of the fillet with one hand and, with your other hand, pinch the protruding tip of the tendon between the backside of a knife blade and your thumb. Pull.

roasting bell peppers

grill method Place whole peppers on a grill over hot coals. Allow the skin closest to the grill to blacken entirely and puff, then rotate 1/4 turn (approximately 2 minutes per turn, depending on heat source). After grilling all the sides, stand each pepper on both ends until they are blackened.

oven broiling method Place whole peppers under a preheated broiler as close as possible to heat without actually touching the heating element. Follow the grill method described above.

sweet potato star stencil

basic recipes
chicken stock
(Makes about 8 cups)

You don't see many bumper stickers proclaiming "I'd rather be making stock." But if you are among the ranks of gourmands who believe that homemade stock is the secret to successful soup, please don't let me stop you.

Once all of the ingredients have been assembled, the stock may be left to simmer on the stove unattended for several hours. Stock may be made in advance and refrigerated for about 3 days, or frozen in small portions for several months. (See the following recipe.) For those of you who prefer to sail, or spend your leisure time in other ways, buy canned stock or broth. Most "real" chefs I know scoff at bouillon cubes (too salty, they say) but many of them recommend the canned variety, and most frequently it's Swanson's. Low-fat and low-salt versions are also available.

3 pounds chicken wings or backs, or a mixture of wings, backs, necks, and giblets (*do not* use livers)
2 medium onions, *peeled and quartered*
2 carrots, *peeled and quartered*
2 bay leaves
10 parsley sprigs
1/2 teaspoon black peppercorns
1/2 teaspoon dried thyme

Rinse the chicken parts under cold running water and add them to a large pot. Add 16 cups of water, making sure that all of the chicken is covered. Bring the water to a boil, then reduce heat to a simmer. Skim the fat and foam from the surface. Add the remaining ingredients to the pot and simmer, without boiling, for 2 to 4 hours, skimming the fat and foam occasionally. Strain the stock through a colander lined with cheesecloth. Discard the solids. Spoon off the fat, cover, and refrigerate for up to 3 days. Remove and discard the congealed layer of fat before reheating.

croutons
(For 6 salad servings)

The best croutons are made from thickly sliced, slightly stale flavorful breads (i.e., sourdough, Italian, and pumpernickel).

4 to 6 thick bread slices, *cut into 3/4-inch cubes*
1/3 cup olive oil
1 garlic clove, *minced* (optional)
2 teaspoons of oregano, thyme, or basil (optional)
2 tablespoons grated Parmesan cheese (optional)

1 Preheat the oven to 350° F.
2 Place the bread in a large bowl, add the oil and any optional ingredients.
3 Toss until the oil is absorbed.
4 Place on a baking sheet or aluminum foil and bake in the oven for about 15 minutes, or until browned. Turn once or twice so that all sides brown evenly.
5 Store in an airtight container.

jalapeño corn bread

(Makes 1 loaf or 12 muffins)

1 cup cornmeal (coarsely ground, if available)
1 cup unbleached all-purpose flour
1/2 teaspoon salt
1 teaspoon baking powder
1/2 teaspoon baking soda
2 tablespoons honey
1 cup buttermilk (or regular whole milk)
2 eggs
2 tablespoons vegetable oil
2 ears fresh corn, *kernels removed and cob discarded*, or 1 cup thawed frozen corn kernels
1 jalapeño or serrano chili, *seeds and membranes discarded, minced*
1/4 cup red bell pepper, *seeds and membranes discarded, finely chopped*
1/2 cup lightly packed fresh cilantro, *coarsley chopped. Remove and discard stems before measuring*

1 Preheat oven to 400° F.
2 Mix the first 5 ingredients together in a medium bowl.
3 In another medium bowl, whisk together the honey, buttermilk, eggs, and oil.
4 Slowly stir the liquid mixture into the dry mixture, blending well.
5 Blend in the corn, chili, bell pepper and cilantro leaves.
6 Pour the mixture into a greased 8-by-4-inch loaf pan, or a tray of muffin cups. Bake the loaf for 25 to 30 minutes, the muffins for 15 to 20 minutes, or until a toothpick inserted in the center comes out clean.

the adventure club   Before adding the corn kernels to the mixture, sauté them in 1 tablespoon of butter over medium high heat for about 10 minutes, or until they begin to brown. This caramelizes the corn, giving it a sweeter, richer flavor.

liquorcabinetlist

(In rough order of popularity)

liquors

Vodka
Gin
Scotch
Tequila
Rum (white)
Rye
Dry vermouth
   (for Martinis)

liqueurs

Brandy
Cognac
Grand Marnier (or Cointreau, my favorite)
Kahlúa
Drambuie
Bailey's Irish Cream

mail-order sources

To order a 12-ounce bottle of Gaucho Jack's Legendary Argentinean Pepper Sauce, send $8, including shipping, to: "Gaucho Jack" Blumer, P.O. Box 4356, Burlington, VT 05406. (Make check payable to "Gaucho" Jack Blumer. Tell him his Surreal son sent you.)

where i learned the things i did not know

Food Lover's Companion (a food dictionary), by Sharon Tyler Herbst (Barron's)
The Wellness Encyclopedia of Food and Nutrition, by Sheldon Margen, M.D. (Rebus)
The Lobster Almanac, by Bruce Ballenger (Globe Pequot)

Elvis cookbooks

Are You Hungry Tonight? Elvis' Favorite Recipes, by Brenda Arlene Butler (Gramercy Books)
Fit for a King: The Elvis Presley Cookbook, by Elizabeth McKeon (Ingram Book Company)
The Life And Cuisine Of Elvis Presley, by David Adler (Crown Paperbacks)

the musical hardware wishlist

the five CD turntable The great $200 party investment. It's the ultimate party DJ. These players allow you to load five CDs at a time, program order or randomness, and spin about 4 hours of continuous music. Of course, it renders the guest DJ's job obsolete. But then that's one more person available to help out in the kitchen.

outdoor speakers If you do a lot of outdoor entertaining, all-weather speakers may be just the ticket. Bose makes a great sounding pair for about $200. For added intrigue, conceal your speakers in the bushes. It is advisable to point them in such a way that the sound is directed at your guests rather than your neighbors.

boom box Let your speakers do the walking. Ideal for a party that moves from room to room, or from inside to outside to inside, and so on.

party help

(Acknowledgments, in alphabetical order)

A sincere thank you to all of my friends and neighbors who endured my transformation into the Surreal-Gourmet-from-hell during the months that I lived and breathed this book. I picked their brains, borrowed everything that wasn't bolted down, and exploited them as culinary guinea pigs. As a testimony to their tolerance, they remained generous with their comments and ideas, many of which are woven throughout these pages. Hey guys, the next party's at my place.

the "A" list
Gina Stepaniuk: purveyor of old-world secrets and new-world aesthetics
Kate Burns: enlightened counsel since our (Caesar) salad days
Kate Sage: "official tester" and unflappable source of sage advice
Mark Collis: Toronto's grooviest chef
Matt Zimbel: kindred cooking spirit and fearless foodie
Norman Perry: source of absolute friendship and infinite wisdom

the chopping board
Charlotte Stone: Surreal editor, rainmaker, and (occasional) baby-sitter
Christopher Bird: writer of wrong, benevolent neighbor, and slobbering dog owner

the zest
Dick Kaiser: photographer extraordinaire, and Surreal springboard
Kevin Reagan: rock-art legend and occasional book designer

green grocers
Doug Mark, Marc Geiger, Robert Phillips

the kitchen cabinet
Allison Wright, Ami Sky & Marc Jordan (formerly Amy & Mark), Carol Marks-George & Chris Dafoe, Cinderella Dietrich, Dean Fearing, Debbie Jow, Heidi "Queen of the Unmonied Elite" Von Palleske, Jackie Moss, Karen Gordon, Liz Janik, Leslie "keeper of the 'B' List" Hollenberg, Louise Adams, Margo McNeeley, Maureen & Pat Doherty, Meesha Halm, Melanie Ciccone, Mimi, Nancy Silverton, Quincy Houghton, Romily Perry, Sandy Gleysteen, Sara Burns, Sarah Blumer & Blair Damson, Shep Gordon, Simone Seydoux

sous-chefs
Bill Bentley, Bob Duscus, Brenda Lazare, Button Hollenberg, Cathy Pullman, Chris Douridas, Cindy Ridgway, Doug "come to my surprise party" Lindeman, Ellen Rose, Felix & Sandra Chamberlain, "Gaucho" Jack Blumer, Jerry Casale, Isabelle Megias-Fox (perpetrator of the grapefruit chicken massacre) Jane Coffey, Janet Grey, Jeff Heiman, Jeff Smith, Joe Henry, Julie Logan, Marjorie Skouris, Margo Burns, Marina Rota, Miguel Salas, Mike Koch, Nancy Walker, Rick Arnstein, Rick Striecker, Rodney Bowes, Sally Shepherd, Sandy Castonguay, Scott Martin, Steve Waxman, Steve Van Wormer (inventor of the fried peanut butter and jam sandwich — not this time Steve, maybe in my next book), Stephen Grynberg, Susan Grode, Suzi "The Worlds Greatest Assistant" Varin, Toby Mamis, Yale Evelev, Yvonne Troxclair, Waldo & Cherry Pesto, Wayne Chick, Zig Gron

the "D" list
Clarissa Troop, Claudia Lloyd, Colleen Woodcock, Kate Farquharson

suppliers
All of the farmers at the Hollywood farmer's market, in front of whose produce I kneel every Sunday morning, Dede & Jon — purvayers of the electric garlic stand, Anchor Hocking, Bell Helmets, Café — the unofficial, official shirt of the Surreal Gourmet, Chic-A-Boom, Messermeister knives, Michael's Art Supplies, Northwest Airlines, The McIlhenny Co., Rick "gets it" Dunn, Utensils - Rachael Fratto

future gourmands
Aisha, Alistair, Caroline, Dylan, Ethan, Gabriella, Hallie, Holly, Levon, Lucas, Oliver, Rylan, Sami, Sophie, Teddy Jr.

v.i.p.s
"All-access" kitchen passes go to: Teddy Moss for sharing a fine glass of wine with the big guy, then toughing it out to come back and drink plonk with us mere mortals; Alison Emilio for her undying confidence; Marshall Rousseau and everyone at the Salvador Dalí Museum, St. Petersburg, FL; and all my pals at Chronicle Books – the coolest, funnest publisher in all the land

entertaining moments to remember

jokes to remember

barenakedinthekitchen?

Wear the fruits and sauces of your labor proudly on a Surreal Gourmet apron. For a list of items for your kitchen that you won't find at the local mall (including aprons, limited-edition silkscreens and photos, original art, and other Surreal collectables), call, write, e-mail or surf to the Surreal mall:

1-800-FAUX-PAS
The Surreal Gourmet, P.O. Box 2961, Hollywood, CA, USA 90078
mall@surrealgourmet.com
HTTP://surrealgourmet.com

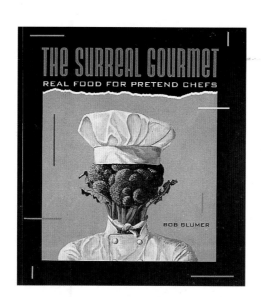

If you have made it to this point without burning down the kitchen, check out
The Surreal Gourmet: Real Food For Pretend Chefs
Also available from Chronicle Books at your favorite store.
To order from the comfort of your own kitchen, call or surf to the Surreal mall (see above).